A Piece of My Mind

Thoughts. Memories. Stories. Dreams

Peter Clothier

A Piece of My Mind

Thoughts, Memories, Stories, Dreams

Peter Clothier

A Piece of My Mind
Thoughts, Memories, Stories, Dreams

Copyright © 2024 Peter Clothier

All Rights Reserved.

The opinions expressed in this manuscript are solely the opinions of the author and do not represent the opinions or thoughts of the publisher. The author has represented and warranted full ownership and/or legal right to publish all the materials in this book. This book may not be reproduced, transmitted, or stored in whole or in part by any means, including graphic, electronic, or mechanical without the express written consent of the publisher except in the case of brief quotations embodied in critical articles and reviews.

ISBN: 979-8-9919296-0-8

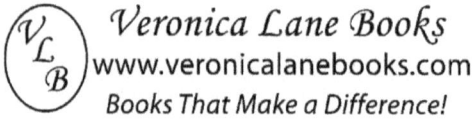

Veronica Lane Books
www.veronicalanebooks.com
Books That Make a Difference!

Veronica Lane Books
11420 US1, Suite 124
N. Palm Beach, FL 33408
1-833-VLBOOKS [1-833-852-6657]

For Ellie

Still, after all these years…!
and what would I ever do
without you?

These pages
dedicated, as always
with all my love.

Acknowledgments

Above all, I am grateful for those who take the time and trouble to read the words I write on social media—the source of most of what this book contains. I am most grateful to the faithful few—those who read frequently and comment, and those who read but do no more than "like", or "care", or "laugh." I am grateful to those who criticize, and argue, and show me where I'm wrong, and make me think again. I am grateful to those who lurk, unknown, behind the scenes, but whose presence is still felt. I am grateful to those who simply stumble in, in search of something else, and stumble off again, wherever interest or whim takes them.

The social media are easy targets for mockery and scorn. They are subject to rightful criticism for their easy access to those who would abuse them. For myself, however, the much-maligned Facebook has proved to be a welcoming and pleasant meeting place for friends and "friends" alike, and I am grateful for the resource it has provided me for what I value most: the ability to make connections with my fellow travelers in this rich, diverse, and sometimes troublesome world that we all love.

PC

There is no pleasure to me without communication: there is not so much as a sprightly thought comes into my mind that it does not grieve me to have produced alone, and that I have no one to tell it to.

- Michel de Montaigne (1533-1592)

Table of Contents

Introduction	1
Not Now	3
Deterioration	5
Body as mansion	8
No complaints	10
Patterns	12
Not Just a Number	14
Normandy	17
A Hare-Brained Scheme	19
Going home	21
Rabbit	25
Pot	28
The Mad Potter	31
Sacred	33
Passing	36
Chicken Little	38
Romcom	40
Our 50th	42
Adorable	45
Insecurity	46
Smile	49
Depression, Part I	50
Radical acceptance	52
Peggy	55
Harry	58
The Windermere children	61
Oppenheimer	64
Doctors	67
Covid	69
Bob went home	71
"My" Ego	74

Alter ego	77
Art Saturday	79
Virtue	81
Change	83
Democracy at Risk	85
Democrats!	88
A Commonsense Manifesto	91
Cri de Coeur	94
Why?	96
The Getty	99
Poor Me	102
Prayer	105
The Lost Art	109
This is Not Me	112
A Nice Story	114
WWBD?	117
November 2015	121
The Internet	124
The Hand	126
My Commencement Speech	130
A Fall	133
Lying	134
The Mute "e"	136
After Las Vegas	139
The Gift of Art	141
Hide, Repress, Deny	143
Apropos	146
Good-Looking	148
Ekphrasis	150
Prejudice	154
Past and Future	156
Overpopulation	160
Always Before	161
The Magic Flute	163
Country Boy	165
Three Boys	168
Tragedy or Farce?	170

The Hardest Job	172
Surgery	174
The Scam	177
Shadow	180
Rosh Hashanah	186
Roses	188
Ricardo	190
Retreat	193
A Critic	196
Bottoms Up	198
School Days	200
Old Friends	203
Men and Cars	205
The Health Spa	208
If You Meet the Buddha	210
My Rage	212
Two Dreams	215
Charlie	218
Hats Off	220
Grief	223
Rhymes	226
Posing Naked	228
Who We Are	230
The Boss	233
Ten of Us	238
Witness	239
Uncouth	242
Bumpkin	245
Purple Ice Cream	247
Doctor, Doctor	249
Headache	251
Wasps	253
A Letter	254
Letting go	256
Spiritual	262
The Fox and the Crow	265
Mondrian	267

In Praise of Modesty	269
Gratitude, Always	271
Expanding Perception	273
Depression, Part II	276
The Dead	278
D-Day	280
Good News!	282
Envoi	285

Introduction

Not for the first time a kind reader has suggested I should think about putting together a collection of the short essays that I post regularly on my social media. I confess I have given the idea some thought myself and am now reconsidering it.

It's too late in life—and perhaps I'm simply too lazy—to go bothering with the agents, editors, publishers, and so on required for a commercial publication. It may seem odd, too—and even though I have been at it since the age of 14 when I published my first poem in a school magazine—that I have always insisted on thinking of myself as an amateur writer. I have made modest sums of money along the way, of course, but that has never been the point. I do it because, as an "amateur", it is what I love to do. In words I often quote from the poet Robert Creeley, it is "what I am given to do". I have no doubt that many, if not most of the artists I have written about must feel the same. I still remember, years later, the enthusiastic reception to an essay I published called *A Word for the Amateur* which I wrote in response to the then ubiquitous art school injunction at all artists must be "professional."

There is a great tradition of what I like to think of, quaintly, perhaps, as "gentlemen writers" (women, forgive me! You are gentle, too, and writers, artists, no less dedicated to your art, and certainly no less accomplished!) in the same spirit as gentlemen farmers. My great heroes in this tradition, mentors, really, all happen to be French, merely because of educational choices that led me to study them in greater depth: Montaigne, Pascal, La Rochefoucauld, Rousseau... from all of whom I learned that it's okay to write about myself, about what's going on in my own life, in my own mind; what makes me human.

I think, too, of my father, Harry, the parish priest. As children, my sister Flora and I knew that we must walk on tiptoe past his study door toward the end of the week; that we must play quietly, discreetly, where we would not be disturbing him in the important work of writing his weekly Sunday sermons. He took them seriously, reading them in his mellifluous voice from the pulpit to an audience of parishioners who, I believe, loved to learn, loved to listen to him.

A modest man who, paradoxically, took great pride in his work, it could never have occurred to Harry to collect and publish them as a book. And yet... how sad that they are forever lost, that there is no record of those hours of labor and love he devoted to their composition. So it is his memory, in part, that has me thinking once again of doing so. Not in the hope of commercial publication. Not in the hope of financial return, obviously. Not in the hope of acclaim or renown. But simply For The Record.

Not Now

As anyone who has embarked on a meditation practice will tell you, the greatest obstacle in your path is the distractions. They come, basically, in three forms: thoughts, physical sensations, and feelings. Of the three, for me at least, the thoughts are the most challenging to deal with. For many others too, it would appear. I can't count the number of friends who have told me they would really like to meditate but their mind is far too busy to allow it.

One of the most common misconceptions about meditation is that it's a blessed time-out from the troubles life brings your way, a mental suspension of brain activity in favor of a kind of mindless blissing out. The concepts of no-self and nirvana are easily misunderstood.

In my experience, the opposite is true. The purpose of meditation is to open and clarify the mind, to awaken it and to make it super alert to the presence and fulness of each passing moment. The distractions come along to make that hard to do. The advice you will get from any teacher is to let them pass; you will hear that if you simply note their presence without getting attached, those distractions will simply and inevitably drift away like clouds.

Anyone who has embarked on a meditation practice will also tell you this is easier said than done. It requires training and skill.

The best advice I ever had on this subject came in the form of two simple words: Not now. It's something you can tell yourself to take refuge from the aches and pains, the feelings that can arise when you're sitting quietly, and the obsessively returning thoughts.

Not now.

Sometimes it works. Sometimes it doesn't.

The passing "Thoughts" in this collection are those that came to me almost exclusively in meditation. When "not now" was successful, I was able to tuck them away somewhere in the back of my mind and mysteriously process them in some unconscious way, allowing them to return later almost verbatim for me to transcribe. When "not now" was not successful, I would sit there pursuing my writing practice instead of my meditation practice, scribbling away in my head to find the words to say exactly what I wanted them to say.

I have shared dozens, scores, and even hundreds of such passing thoughts on social media or blogs. I claim no originality for them, nor even great significance, but I have lately found myself wishing for them not to waft away forever, lost in the virtual space of the amorphous "cloud." Here they are, some of them, in no particular order, chosen only because, on re-reading, they still speak to me in some way. Do not look for any logical sequence, it does not exist. Together, I like to think, they constitute the portrait of one human being simply trying to make sense of the vicissitudes of life and to find his place, with his fellow human beings, in an often confusing and sometimes alienating world. They have been a welcome refuge for their author. I share them in the hope that a reader will also find in them some refuge.

Deterioration

I have been thinking about deterioration. About how the body deteriorates with age. About how the hips and knees that have carried my weight around for so many years begin to give out under me. About those things that came easily to me not so long ago—like stooping to pick up a piece of paper that I've dropped, like pulling up my socks or putting on a pair of shoes—become a physical challenge that can seem insurmountable. About how in the plumbing system—I speak for myself and other men because this is a shared masculine experience—what was once a reliably sturdy flow becomes a pathetic, often painful dribble. About how the whole body lets me know when I've asked too much of it and responds with aches and pains from top to toe. Even the simple act of getting in and out of bed can require previously unimaginable effort.

So there's that. But then the heart and brain deteriorate in the same way. Those little flaws in the emotional make-up that were once no more than the source of occasional irritation or embarrassment become glaring deficiencies of character. If I tended, in my younger years, to be introspective, private, and quiet, I find myself in age becoming a crochety hermit, easily bruised by contact with even those closest to me. If a person was once timid, she is now a little mouse. If a man was loud and brash and rude, self-confident, and ambitious, those qualities morph into the implacable demands of the aging tyrant. What were once little vulnerabilities for which one could compensate or readily disguise become the open wounds you must now defend fiercely from attack or exploitation.

As for the brain, I can attest to the deplorable certainty that it will no longer function as it used to. It is well known that brain cells die. Millions of them every day, I hear. Could that be right? It's hard to keep all this information straight. As everyone knows, the failing short-term memory is the first and most obvious thing to go. You can't remember where you left the car keys just a few minutes ago and spend useless hours searching for them in a panic. You meet a friend you've known for years and even if you recognize her face—sometimes problematic in itself—you can't for the life of you recall her name.

Or, quick now, what did you have for dinner last night?

But memory is not the only problem. It's the ability to listen, concentrate, read, analyze, digest. Even simple arithmetic becomes a challenge. Your brain checks out even as you're listening to the person talking to you or watching a show on television. You try hard to follow the argument, and the plot line, but it eludes you. Tiring of the effort, the brain decides that it's not worth all the bother and you quietly nod off. Try to explain some meaningful concept or describe an event to a friend and you'll see what I mean. You find yourself searching for words that adamantly refuse to come. Telling a story is easier because it matters little if you lose track or forget the point; it's fun to wander. Besides, your listener has probably heard it from you a dozen times before.

Did I hear a mention of that word, wisdom? Hmmm. It's a flattering euphemism we indulge in because it turns our simple-mindedness into an asset. We like to think that our wisdom allows us greater insight because accurate perception has become a challenge. A foggy mind is unperturbed by detail, and it's surely true that too much analysis, too much obsession with irrelevant detail can obscure what's otherwise simple, evident and true.

Because we speak slowly, we are presumed to be delving into a fount of sagacity accessible only to those who have accumulated the requisite number of years. Would that it were so. We are speaking slowly because we can't think as fast and clearly as we used to.

I know I've said nothing here that is new or original. I myself have said it all before. But how to cope with all this? How to age, as they say, gracefully? A sense of humor is important, certainly—the ability to stand back and have a good laugh at your too easily deflated ego. A sense of perspective, an understanding that we are not alone in the experience of growing old. An acknowledgment and acceptance of our predicament. Most of all, though, a healthy dose of tolerance, patience, kindness, and compassion—towards ourselves as well as others. An ability to breathe it in and breathe it out, and to allow the necessary healing to take place somewhere in between the breaths.

I hope to be able to show, in the passing thoughts that follow, how this is a skill available to anyone who cares to make the time to learn it—although the most important thing to learn is that the learning never stops.

Body As Mansion

I have been playing recently, as I sit in meditation, with the body-as-mansion metaphor. Down in the sub-basement are the plumbing and the sewers; in the lower belly, the kitchens and pantries; and above, in the upper belly, the servants' quarters; around the midriff is the living area, with sitting rooms and studies, the library; the solar plexus, if you will, is the conservatory. The great bedrooms are located in the chest and the attic is the head, with its trunksful of old memories, the stuff of ages. The brain is what I like to think of as the children's playroom, always busy with the noise of silly games. The eyes, of course, the windows, the limbs, the stairways, and the corridors, their steps and floorboards creaking as you age...

You can play around with all these spaces any way you want. It's fun. But the point is this: the prime purpose of meditation, as I see it, is to clear the mind, get rid of the accumulated rubble and debris, the dust and cobwebs, clean the windows, make the beds, polish the floors and do the dishes, and leave the place pristine. In scanning through the body, you can find trace evidence of all those things that distract and clutter the mind, the ever-wandering thoughts and memories, the ghosts of the past and future plans. You find them in the physical sensations, the aches and pains, the desires, revulsions, nauseas; and last—not least!—the passing feelings, fear, and anger in the belly or the heart, sadness, even bursts of joy. Distractions, all.

It's a useful experiment, to explore the body-as-mansion. Think Downton Abbey! Above all, it's salutary to start the process of spring cleaning. Try washing the windows first. Think of polishing the scales from the eyes. Only then can you see out over the cultivated gardens, the green lawns and lakes, and, beyond, the hills and mountains. And above them, the endless sky and the infinitude of space.

Exhilarating! You'll find yourself seeing with new eyes.

No Complaints

I was happy to be able to join my sitting group in Laguna Beach last Sunday. I am able to go too rarely these days, now that Ellie and I must often stay in Los Angeles for medical reasons. In normal times, before Covid, before Ellie's year-long bout with cancer, before broken bones and hip replacements (two of them!) I would go every Sunday for an hour's silent meditation, followed usually by an hour's friendly discussion of whatever was on our minds. I joined the group more than twenty years ago, and it has been one of the important anchors in my life. Another refuge.

I always come away having learned something of importance, and this past Sunday was no exception. One of our fellow sitters was just back from a 700-mile hike along the Continental Divide Trail and regaled us with many fascinating stories of the delights and rigors of that great challenge to human endurance. Deserts and prairies, rushing streams to cross, and mountains to climb with still deep remaining snow from the winter storms in New Mexico. He told us of great beauty… and great hardship all at once.

There is, our friend also told us, a wonderful spirit of companionship amongst the hikers, who come from all parts of the world. He spoke about the culture of the hiking community and, when asked to elaborate, about the most important common agreement among hikers: no complaints. No matter how long or painful the day's walk, no matter how aching the joints or how sore the feet, no matter how heavy the backpack or how scarce the supplies, no one complains. It's just not done.

Our friend's story left me thinking about my own comfortable life—and how often I hear myself complaining! I slept too little or too long. My left hip aches, my right hip is not yet fully recovered from the latest replacement surgery. My telephone rings too often with junk calls. The Los Angeles traffic is unbearable; most of the drivers never learned to drive and shouldn't be on the road. The inversion layer from the ocean clouds the blue sky and blocks the sun. There are endless reasons for complaint. I'm sure you have your own list; it might even include some of mine.

And then I think, how graceless! As I listened to our hiking friend, I was invited to recognize how petty and ungracious is my own list of complaints—I, who have in reality so little to complain about and how much to be grateful for. I set the intention to start watching myself with greater attention and to call myself out when I catch myself complaining about the little things. Or even about the big ones. I have been thinking about the wisdom of stoicism and the common ground between that philosophy and the Buddhist dharma. It is a worldview that is little known or valued in our contemporary culture; I have a book by Marcus Aurelius—a gift from my son!—and it is now at the top of my pile of books I mean to read. And I think once more with a kind of veneration of an old friend and mentor (not literally: I'm not quite that old!) Michel de Montaigne, whose *"Essais"* were first published in 1580 and continue to provide me with the inspiration and model for everything I write. The adage for which he is best known is this: "*Que sçai-je?*"

What do I know?

I write, as this literary giant did so many years ago, for this reason: to find out.

Patterns

I believe that each of us has a unique structure of visual organization. I also believe that whatever structure we have is the result of the visual character of the place in which we spent our earliest years. Each of us sees with our own pattern, but artists and gardeners are the ones to find that pattern and build something that we can see around it.

- Gregory Conniff

This quotation caught my eye. It arrived as one in the series of images called "The Power of Photography" that I have been receiving for a long while now—I believe since the onset of the coronavirus—from Peter Fetterman's photography gallery. I always look at the images when they arrive, usually with a quotation of this kind from the artist or some other appropriate source, and they are always of interest, sometimes provocative. This one resonated strangely, without my quite understanding why.

For me, the place in which I spent my earliest years is the small village of Aspley Guise in Bedfordshire, where my family moved when I was barely 2 years old, and as Conniff suggests, the visual memories of that place have always haunted my imagination. I suspect, without quite understanding how it applies to my work as a writer, that this is the source of my "unique structure of visual organization" and that it manifests in some mysterious way in everything I write.

Writing is not obviously a visual art, but what I write is almost always based in image as well as language and I often hear from readers about the visual quality that results. I do believe, with Conniff, that there are structures of the mind that are created very early in our lives, and that they govern much of what we create—whether as artists and photographers or as writers. It is significant for me that my first publication—a chapbook of poems—was entitled *Aspley Guise*, and that the poems powerfully evoke images of St. Botolph's church and the Rectory that were the center of my life.

I may not fully "understand" what Conniff is saying here, but that does not prevent his words from resonating at some deep level of my consciousness. For me, they have the mystery of poetry, words that can be grasped without rational understanding and are sufficient in themselves. Their structure is often buried in internal rhythms and rhymes we do not stop to notice, in the way lines break, and the silences of white space around them—which is where their "meaning" lies.

As I pursue the exploration of my mind and its inner workings in meditation, I appreciate the perception that Conniff's words bring to illuminate my practice. There is always more to learn, always a deeper level of understanding to be reached...

Not Just A Number

I get a little tired of all the happy talk around age. Forgive me if it's your favorite adage, but "It's just a number" rankles me, as do bromides like "You're as old as you feel", "80 is the new 60", and so on. The platitudes are well intended, surely—though let's not forget that there is an issue of social privilege here—and it's true that many of us carry our age well these days. It's remarkable that modern medical advances and accepted cultural norms (again, social privilege!) like maintaining a healthy diet and exercise program make it possible for people to live well into their 90s and even 100s in great shape, both mentally and physically. Good for them. I'm all for it. Still, the familiar pleasantries about age ring hollow in the ears of the many, perhaps even the most among us who are not so blessed and serve only to arouse feelings of guilt or envy, shame, or embarrassment for somehow having flunked the age test, for not being as youthful and spry and sharp-witted as we are supposed to be.

I land somewhere in the middle of all this. In so many ways, I count myself among the blessed. Here I am, approaching my 88th birthday and my body continues to serve me as well. My heart continues to beat with reliable regularity, as it has done every minute of every hour since my original birthday. Which is amazing. I have a replaced hip on both sides now, and a knee that keeps reminding me it's time to get a new one. But… I can walk! I can see pretty well, thanks to cataract surgery. I can hear just fine. (Ellie disputes this claim, but I insist that my hearing lapses are a matter of choice, not malfunction!) My brain functions adequately, though perhaps not quite so deftly as it used to. It takes more time to react, and while my memory is not as sharp as it once was, I like to think that I'm not dotty yet. I have a full head of hair, unlike my father whose hair had significantly thinned by this age. It is silver, yes, and has been for some years, but still growing apace. I already need another haircut and it has only been about three weeks. (How many haircuts, I wonder, have I had? Maybe six or eight a year, times 87... I'm not going to bother with the math). I have not lost my sense of purpose or my passion: I sit with my laptop almost every day and pound out the words. Well, I used to pound: in my early years, I worked on a typewriter, which required pounding. These days a light tap is enough on the computer keyboard—but I still miss the clackety-clack.

So yes, I am fortunate, even though the body keeps reminding me that age can't be shrugged off with clichés. Why should I deny it? The spring has gone from my walk. The plumbing is clogged by the enlarged prostate that every man can expect with age. I suffer from various vexing ailments, enough to make a significant contribution to that familiar "organ recital" when I get together with my peers. Pain is a constant companion. I have concluded that it will be with me for the rest of my life, so I need to make friends with it; if not, I will be in a constant state of struggle and denial. The effort to pretend otherwise only aggravates it, while simple acceptance denies me the right to moan and groan. It is (to use that useful current cliché!) what it is. I can get ahead with the important things in life without the added burden of a fruitless and unending effort—in the words of the serenity prayer—to change what I cannot change.

So it all comes down to acceptance, which will allow me, I hope, to submit gracefully to the ravages of age as and when they come. I may need to learn to accept the care of others, much against my nature. Acceptance is itself a form of grace.

I find it important, then, to acknowledge that age is more than just a number. Rather, it is a reality to be embraced for its privileges as well as for its undesirable accompanying effects. It's my intention to keep feeling exactly as old as I am, not a day older, not a day younger. For now, I accept with gratitude the good intentions of those who think to compliment me when they say I don't look a day over 60, or who assure me that I'm "looking good", even if "for your age" remains unspoken. But I don't take them seriously. I find instead that, in honoring my age, I am far more able to enjoy it.

Normandy

Ellie and I like to watch the CBS Sunday Morning show, a TV magazine that always has something of interest and mercifully abstains from the dire news of the day. It devotes a few seconds at the end to a brief video of some beautiful natural environment with—or without!—birds or animals doing what birds and animals do. Always too short, these final shots are a welcome invitation to remember what is truly important. Yesterday, the day before Memorial Day, they chose to show images of the beaches at Normandy, including a few glimpses of the cemetery where the bodies of so many brave men are laid to rest.

In those long, slow shots, the beaches and the quiet lines of the waves breaking on the shore seemed so pacific, contrasting with the constant roar and turmoil of the winds. Watching, I was once again inspired by the incredible bravery of those men leaping off their landing craft into the cold waters—and the hail of bullets from Nazi machine guns on the bluffs overlooking their easy, virtually defenseless targets. Once more I tried to imagine the unimaginable fear those men must have had to somehow overcome, to wade through the breakers and onto the sand toward the expectation of imminent death. Once more I wonder if I would have been able to muster that courage, had I been of an age to serve, rather than the eight years old I was at the time.

It's Memorial Day today. Curiously, Ellie and I met on Memorial Day and got married a few years later on Armistice Day, 11/11. Veteran's Day this side of the pond. I think of those brave men who died on the Normandy beaches, with gratitude and awe. Did they think, as they leaped off their barges, of the higher purpose they were serving: to save Europe and the world from the affliction of tyranny? I suspect their minds were on less lofty thoughts like plain, animal survival. Today's familiar cliché, "Thank you for your service", rings hollow from the lips of people like me who never had to serve on the battlefield. The best, most honest way to thank them is to follow their example, fighting back with fierce determination whenever tyranny threatens us again.

Which happens, sadly, here as in so many other parts of the world, to be this very moment.

A Hare-Brained Scheme

How's this for a hare-brained scheme? (What is with hares and their brains anyway? Are they daft?) I'm flying to England for the weekend to take Georgia, my granddaughter, to tea at the college where she followed me by sixty years.

It's not quite that simple. I leave Thursday from Los Angeles International, arrive on Friday at Heathrow, have that tea with my granddaughter on Saturday, spend Sunday with my son and daughter-in-law and as many of their three children as can be assembled, and fly back to LAX on Monday.

It happened this way: the day before yesterday I received an email invitation from my old Cambridge college, Gonville & Caius (we abbreviate it to Caius and—this being England—pronounce it "Keys". It was founded in 1348 and named after its co-founder, Dr. John Caius). The email extended an invitation to attend a May Week Party with a guest. May Week, of course—this being England—is in the middle of June, and it celebrates the Bumps, the annual boat races between the colleges, so-called because the river is too narrow for two boats to race side-by-side. The victor is decided by "bumping" the boat ahead. I think I have that right. I was no oarsman as my father Harry was, also at Caius, a hundred years ago. I mean that literally. He was "up", as we say, in the 1920s, and I followed him in the 1950s. It's a family thing.

Or so it was when I matriculated. In those days heredity still counted; I have often wondered whether I was good enough to have been admitted without the patrimonial tradition. But thankfully I was and spent three wonderful years at Cambridge trying to grow up (I did not succeed) and working towards a degree in Modern and Medieval Languages and French Philology (at which I did succeed, but barely). But I know for sure that this tradition was no longer a factor when Georgia was admitted four years ago to read (Cambridge for "study") Linguistics—a much more demanding version of Philology. By this time that dubious old tradition had been properly superannuated: Georgia was admitted on her own substantial merits.

So there it was, the invitation. A ridiculous idea. I slept on it Friday night and woke on Saturday morning with the foolish notion that I should accept it. I consulted Ellie. Graciously, she encouraged my wild idea. I called my son Matthew, who happened at that moment to be in the South of France and consulted with him and his wife, Diane, who these days live not far from Cambridge. The dates worked for them. Everything was falling into place. I called Georgia to propose the idea. She seemed surprised, unsurprisingly, but surprisingly pleased. I called United Airlines and bought myself a business class ticket—with a full-length, lie-down seat—on the strength of bonus miles left unused in the three years since Covid. Before two hours were up, it was all perfectly arranged.

That was the easy part. Now comes the hard part: I have to actually do it. I must admit to a certain trepidation. I am not young (I thought of this as an 87th birthday present to myself) and my joints ache. My brain is still functional, however, though "hare-brained" seems an accurate description of my plan. The rest of me will surely recover after jet lag. I have six weeks to prepare. And it will be, I reassure myself, an adventure…

Going Home

> *Home is where one starts from*
> —T. S. Eliot, "East Coker: The Four Quartets, Part II*

Remember ET? OK, cheap-seat philosophy at best, But I've been thinking about this extraterrestrial's very terrestrial yearning to go home. So, yes, I did go home. The long flight from Los Angeles to Heathrow was made easy by the luxury of my business class seat, and I arrived in good shape to spend just three days in my native land with my son and his family before coming back home which is, these days, Los Angeles. It was literally to be what they call a flying visit.

It was in the context of the experience of being back in England that my son Matthew and I got to talking one evening about the meaning of coming home. Perhaps because of my accent, I am often asked where I come from; after more than sixty years in North America (I came first to Canada in 1962). Still, after all these years, my speech patterns and intonation are stuck somewhere in the middle of the Atlantic. Sometimes the question is more specific: what part of England do you come from? My answer always starts, "Well, I was born in the North..." And yes, in fact, I was born in Newcastle-on-Tyne and am still absurdly proud to call myself a Geordie, even though I spent only the first year-and-a-half of my life in that part of the world and returned only once, on a brief drive-through on my way to Edinburgh. A Geordie, by the way, is anyone born on the banks of the River Tyne, in the same way that a Cockney is born within the sound of Bow Bells. So I always say that Newcastle is "where I come from" even though I do not have the distinctive accent. As real English people are quick to point out: "You don't sound like a Geordie."

Matthew knows what I'm talking about because he has a similar experience. He was born in Halifax, Nova Scotia. Though he lived there for as little time as I in Newcastle—the family moved to the United States soon after he was born and he lived here in the US until leaving for a fifteen-year residence in Japan in his early twenties—he still thinks of himself as Canadian. He has a Canadian passport.

In times past, most people spent their entire lives where they came from. You lived in that one place, surrounded by your family, your tribe, your clan. There was never a thought of going anywhere else. The Industrial Revolution made the difference; people started leaving their native villages, migrating to big cities to find work in the factories. Toward the end of the 19th century, they began emigrating to distant countries in search of a better life, leaving kith and kin behind. This great deracination has been accelerating ever since, today on a global scale thanks to climate changes and attendant crop failures, famine, and drought. Vast numbers of people are no longer able to maintain a living where they come from.

I suspect there are many people reading these words who know precisely what I'm talking about. Moving from place to place is now commonplace, and yet there is something in the human heart—certainly in my heart—that continues to long for "home." It was Pliny the Elder, Google tells me, who wrote, "Home is where the heart is." I have "a" home here in Los Angeles. I use quotation marks not to disparage it because it is a lovely home, comfortable, welcoming, filled with memories, and with the paintings and art objects Ellie and I have accumulated over our many years together.

Still, when I look out from our balcony over Hollywood and the Hollywood Hills, I know in my heart that even after more than fifty years on this same hill, it is not "home"—where the heart is—but "a home" which is where I live.

It is a whole different feeling driving through the English countryside in what are called the "home counties", because they are those closest to London, the capital. It was in this part of the country that I spent my childhood years, in my father's village parishes in Bedfordshire, Hertfordshire, Buckinghamshire. It is a landscape dotted with small, close-knit communities, each distinguished at the horizon by its church spire or tower, a landscape of low green hills and hedgerows, woods, and farmyards freshened by the frequent rains, of small, rippling streams and grandly flowing rivers. Even for a long-time exile such as myself, the feeling when you return is one of belonging, of being finally home, somehow safe, and recognized, as it were, by the trees themselves, and the birds, and the wildflowers—I am being fanciful, I know—as if I were myself a part of the landscape, and no longer longing, deep in my heart, to be somewhere other than where I am.

It's strange. You do not even have to be born or to have spent your childhood years in a particular place to feel that it is home. I often think that Ellie, born and raised in Los Angeles, has that same deep relationship with New York City, where her grandparents and parents lived until they came west. Unless I'm mistaken, there's a hidden place in her heart where she feels the same call from New York that I feel from the English countryside. We are all—no, forgive me—we are so many of us exiles, deracinated, pulled up from our roots and transplanted, I don't know… elsewhere.

So it's not just calling home, like ET. Home also calls, at least in my experience. Once there I feel reconnected. I leave my daily worries behind me as I settle back into a sense of freedom, of pure rightfulness. I am back home, where I belong.

There is something else, a shadow that haunts me in the dark recesses of consciousness, a place so intimate and secret I scarcely dare to mention it. It is a deeply buried wish to go home to die. I know it is unrealizable, impractical, an ancient fragment of instinct or memory, as in stories of animals that manage this feat—salmon that swim upstream to the place where they were spawned; elephants, they say, though this is a myth that has largely been discredited. I think it is more likely a human wish, projected onto creatures whose native wisdom we intuit without yet understanding. But that deep desire is something that I recognize in myself, a faint echo rising from the depths of the unconscious mind.

I think my sister, Flora, came close. Still sorely missed, she died several years ago, and her body was returned to the earth in the English countryside. We buried her in a simple wicker basket, beneath a fruit tree on a green hillside not unlike the orchard behind the Rectory where we would pick fruit together, brother and sister, in our early years. Unlike her brother, the exile, Flora always returned to her home in England from her travels throughout the world.

There is a history of speaking about dying as "going home," as though our life were no more than a passing visit in a foreign land. It's an appealing concept, even to one who rejects belief in an afterlife, or even a beforelife. It offers a kind of solace, if you need it, in the face of the plain truth of our mortality as human beings. In my head, I understand it as a metaphor. In my heart, I acknowledge it as a profoundly human yearning for the completion of the cycle of our lives.

Rabbit

This morning, reader, get your handkerchief out. It's the sad story of a rabbit. No, it's not what you're thinking. This is not a real, living rabbit, a furry bunny such as children love to hold, or one that scurries off into the undergrowth when you're walking in the woods.

No, this was an artifact, a rabbit fashioned by skilled human hands. It was perhaps twelve inches tall, if you include the pricked-up ears, and it was sitting on its haunches, forelegs dangling, gazing out peacefully into space through jeweled eyes. It was made of silver, heavy, exquisitely crafted, so lifelike you were tempted to stroke it—and were surprised, when you touched it, by its cold metal surface. Its head swung open at the neck, making it a vessel of some kind, though I'm not sure what it was designed to contain. It was too big for perfume. Wine? But challenging to pour. Flowers? You'd have to leave the head hanging back, behind, which would look a bit ridiculous. I have seen it described as a "pitcher," but it had no handle and no lip, so that makes little sense to me.

But there it was, beautiful. Enchanting. And oh, and did I mention it was valuable? I'm talking Fabergé.

I had admired this rabbit for many years in its niche at Ellie's parents' home and I knew just a little of its history. It belonged originally to Ellie's stepmother's mother, a wealthy New York socialite, supporter of the opera (and formerly married to a tenor of some repute), and a lifelong friend of Rose Kennedy. She brought the rabbit back with lots of other knickknacks from a trip to pre-Revolution Russia. I always loved this beautiful object and when Ellie's stepmother died, now decades ago, it passed into my hands by consent of the family, I think—though I could be misremembering—as a reward for stepping up to help with liquidating the estate. It became my most prized possession and sat prominently for many years on a corner of the buffet in our dining room.

Then I sold it. It still feels like a betrayal. We had given the rabbit a home for many years and now filthy lucre stepped in; I simply abandoned the poor creature to an unknown fate. It must have made sense to me at the time. Like most couples, we had our share of financial challenges along the way and the rabbit sat there offering a tempting—although, in retrospect, a purely temporary—solution to a moment of need. So I sold it. I have forgotten how much money was involved. It seemed like a substantial sum at the time (these things are relative) but I'm sure it was less than a Fabergé rabbit was worth. It was certainly much, much less than it was worth to me. To Ellie too, although I always thought of it, selfishly, as *my* rabbit.

I have thought of that rabbit many times in the decades that have passed by since I sold it. I still miss it. Whatever money we got for it was never enough to fill the hole it left in my heart. The moral of the story, surely, is that nothing ever really belongs to us; like it or not, we must learn to let everything go, even those things that seem most permanent, such a lasting presence in our lives. Even the big things. Even this house we live in, perched on the hillside overlooking the city of Hollywood and the Hollywood Hills. Soon enough, someone else will be living here, thinking of it as theirs. And soon enough after that, it will pass into still other hands. In a century, who knows if it will still exist. The big earthquake we have been long expecting could send it tumbling down the hillside. A new owner of the property might decide to tear it down and build a new home of their own design.

We like to think we own, but we own nothing. I was more than fortunate to "own" my rabbit before it went its way. I hope that it found a fine new home where it is appreciated as much as it was for the duration of its stay with me. In any event, inanimate as it is, I can imagine it continuing its journey for many more years than I have left on earth.

Pot

There's a sequel to my previous story about the Fabergé rabbit, but you won't need your handkerchief for this one.

It was many years ago, in the early 1970s, that Ellie and I first embarked on what would become a nearly obsessive hunt for what is known in the collectibles trade as American art pottery. Most of it dates from immediately before and soon after the turn of the 20th century. Both of us had established professional lives in the field of contemporary art, so we considered it a conflict to buy the artwork that Ellie sold, and I wrote about for national magazines. We did discover, though, that we were both bitten by the collecting bug—something Ellie inherited from her parents—and stumbled into this way to keep it satisfied.

It started when Ellie came home with three small matte green vases, just a few inches tall, whose molded Art Deco forms had caught her eye in a nearby antique shop. She had paid just a few dollars for them, but the discovery started us off on a treasure hunt that provided us with endless weekend opportunities for fun. Back then, in the early 1970s, the keen-eyed swap meet or garage sale enthusiast could pick these things out from the rest of the junk and buy them for a relatively trivial sum, so the hobby also fit within our limited budget. Inspired, too, by art world friends like the artist Fidel Danieli and Bob Smith, who directed the fledgling Los Angeles Institute of Contemporary Art, we had plenty of competition for the best finds. The names soon became familiar: Fulper, Rookwood, Roseville,

Weller... But our main focus was what Ellie had originally found, the pottery whose matte green glaze and elegant shapes we loved. Teco—short for the Terra Cotta Company of Chicago—was the brand, and some of its most appealing architectural forms reflected the Prairie style of early 20th-century Midwestern architects. Even Frank Lloyd Wright designed for them.

We searched for these objects everywhere, delighting when we found them. The cost was usually no more than $15 or $20—though once, on a trip to New York City, I spotted a beautiful piece in an antique shop window and went in to ask the price. I was appalled to learn that it was $300! Ridiculous, I thought. It was a largish piece, unusual in design, and in perfect condition. Still, who would ever pay that kind of money for a piece of Teco? Soon afterwards I was waiting in the boarding area at JFK for my flight home when United Airlines started offering $100 and a seat on the next flight in return for a ticket on my overbooked flight. $100? Ridiculous! But moments later they were offering $200. I told myself, half-joking, that if the offer went up to $300, I'd take the money, grab a cab back into the city, buy the Teco, and be back in time for the next flight. Which is how I came to spend $300 on a superb piece of pottery. It still sits amidst the nearly 50 other pieces on our Teco shelves today, and it makes for a great dinner table story.

But this was not the story I started out to tell. By the end of the 1980s, in one of those unpredictable shifts of public taste, prices for American art pottery had begun to soar. A dealer (I will not name him; the art business attracts its share of crooks and I regret to say that this one later spent some time in jail...) who was acquiring special art objects for wealthy Hollywood celebrities approached us about a rather spectacular piece in our collection and offered us a staggering price for it. Our first reaction was to scoff at the offer. But then we had second thoughts. Our car was getting old and was in need of expensive mechanical attention... and the dealer's offer was substantial enough to allow us to buy a new one. Our interest had already settled on a nice new Acura Legend in British racing green whose sticker price exactly matched what we were offered for the Teco.

So we agreed to sell. Ellie insisted on cash, uncertain whether she could trust such an outrageous deal, and the dealer showed up at our house with $15,000 in $100 bills. It seemed a bit shady, but the money was good and we headed off to the Acura dealership with a briefcase stuffed with banknotes. Ellie could hardly wait to settle the deal so she could flash the cash and tell the dealer that the money came from her sale of "pot"! He was unimpressed. Perhaps most of his sales here in downtown Los Angeles were financed by drugs. In any event, our money was accepted in green form, and we drove home in our new Acura Legend, which would serve us well for many years to come.

I never missed that piece of Teco in the same way that I missed my rabbit. True, it had been the biggest and best piece in our collection, and we had stretched our budget to pay $200 for it years before, the most we had ever paid for a piece of Teco aside from my $300 New York City splurge. Lest I leave you with the wrong idea, however, let me add that the American Art Pottery market began to plummet after that banner year of 1989, and today our treasures are worth little more than the pittance we originally paid for them. Such are the vagaries of the art and antiques markets. There's no predicting what will attract the eye of buyers from one year to the next, and the smart collector will not make choices based on investment. What you pay a thousand dollars for this year might be "worth" a hundred next. Or it might be worth ten thousand. There's no telling. The smart collectors are those who buy what they love, and only because they love it. That way you can never go wrong.

Unless, of course, you happen to fall out of love. Which happens.

The Mad Potter

I have just one more pottery tale while it's on my mind. This one is quickly told and requires not even the flimsiest of tissues.

It happened this way: Ellie and I had always loved the eccentric creations of the magnificently mustachioed George Ohr, the Mad Potter of Biloxi—as did any number of other collectors who could better afford to buy his work than we could. The noted artist Jasper Johns, for instance, was a big collector, who often included images of Ohr's pottery in his paintings. Back in our treasure-hunting days, we would occasionally stumble on an affordable example of his extravagant, wildly distorted, sometimes explicitly erotic pots, and the discovery was always a big thrill.

I no longer recall where it was—at the big Rose Bowl swap meet, perhaps, in Pasadena?—we happened on a beautiful George Ohr pot with a lustrous blue-green glaze that we could not resist despite what was, for us, an unusual expense. It became a treasured part of our collection, and remained so until the day when that previously mentioned dealer of questionable repute stopped by to ask if we would be willing to part with it. He had a buyer who was interested, he said, would offer a good price. Well, it happened that at the time, quite untypically for me, my eye had been tempted by a certain rather ancient, rather elegant cherry red Mercedes sedan that was up for sale by the brother of a friend down in Laguna Beach. I will admit to having always been rather skeptical of Mercedes, which triggered not only all my snobbish disparagement of tokens of wealth and luxury but also, I'm sure, a load of totally irrational memories of ancient national enmities between Germany and my native country. Still, this car appealed to me for equally irrational reasons.

The owner was asking $5,000 for this relic. The offer our pottery dealer friend came by with was exactly $5,000 for our beautiful George Ohr pot—for which we had certainly paid less than $50. It seemed like a fair deal. The upshot: for several years thereafter, I was the ridiculously proud owner of a beautiful cherry red Mercedes sedan. It did have a certain undeniable elegance, but its diesel engine also generated an inordinate amount of noise and, absent power steering, the car handled with all the dexterity of a battle tank. For these and a host of other reasons, the initial glow of ownership rather soon wore off, and I was not unhappy when the opportunity arose to trade it back in a couple of years later.

We still have four George Ohr pieces in our collection, fine examples of what he affectionately called his "mud babies"—unglazed forms that miraculously survived the dreadful fire that destroyed his studio in Biloxi in 1894, along with so much of his quirky, irreplaceable work. And this, I promise, will be the last of my pot stories.

Sacred

I like the word "sacred." I use it comfortably. I avoid the word "holy," even though its meaning is very close, precisely because I am not comfortable using it.

What is the difference? To be sacred, nothing needs to be holy. To be holy, at least in my lexicon, an object, person, relationship, or situation requires the sanction of religious faith—and I have not yet found the faith I am able to commit to. I observe a similar difference between adoration and worship. I can adore someone or something without worshipping him or her—or it. To worship, I must believe.

I believe that a relationship can be sacred. It implies the utmost respect, a commitment of the heart, an unshakeable compact between two or more people, a commitment broken only at considerable karmic cost. Such a relationship can, of course, be blessed by religion by those who so choose. But to be sacred it need not be.

Any object can be sacred. A tree. A stone. A ring. A bed shared by two human beings. I don't know, a loaf of bread, a meal. Again, it implies profound respect for the qualities we attribute to it, which may or may not be the same for you as for me, and a commitment never to violate or abuse it. That loaf of bread, for instance. If it is sacred to me, I will not waste it. I will not abuse it with my greed or selfishness. If I do not see it to be sacred, it matters little other than as mere sustenance. I eat it merely out of the need to eat...

The image of the flag occurs to me. Some people choose to see their national flag as sacred—the Union Jack, the Stars and Stripes, and so on. I happen not to. I see it as a symbol, certainly, but not as an object of worship that requires patriotic salutation or belief in a quasi-religious set of notions around the country—and often, yes, a God! It would feel alien, even untrue to me to hold my hand over my heart and swear allegiance to a flag. I recall my horror when I learned that Americans—even children!—were required to do it as an article of faith.

No flag is sacred in my life. I would not choose to burn one, but out of respect for others rather than any sense of sacrilege

An idea can be sacred if held to with that same respect, commitment, and refusal to violate. It too can be religious but is not necessarily so.

Art can be sacred. It need not be. It can also be religious.

There are certain things in my life that I hold sacred. Most of them, but by no means all, are relationships with other human beings. Those I have violated along the way—and there have been some because I am a human being, foolish and fallible, and sometimes weak, and all too often selfish! — have left their mark on my conscience and my psyche. They have left me more than ever respectful of the relationships that bless and illuminate my later years, and more profoundly committed to them.

These days I know that my life would be a poor one without a place for the sacred. Some would argue that I am still searching for religion, that I am dancing on the heads of pins with my little obsessions with verbal niceties. That may be so, but I would argue in return that I feel perfectly content without religion in my life. I am perfectly happy without belief in either the before- or the afterlife that religions were invented to provide as consolation for our inarguable mortality. Even without religion, I can hold and nurture the sacred in my heart.

There. I have written my Sunday sermon. I long ago abandoned my father's Christian beliefs but for many years, as I child, I knew to tiptoe near his study when he was engaged in the important work of sermon writing; and for many years I listened from my seat in the Rector's pew as he preached to his congregation from the pulpit. It is only now, so many years later, that I have come to realize how much I owe to him, and how much he passed on to me of his skill with words and his sense of their importance. I am not so much unlike him after all.

Passing

In the context of my thoughts about the words "sacred" and "holy", it occurred to me to note down a few observations about a related euphemism that I have never cared for—the easy glossing over of the unpalatable reality of death and dying with the notion of "passing"—or "passing over" or, worse in my view, "transitioning."

The subject came up recently with a close friend who had just lost someone especially dear to her. (There I go again! "Lost"! Another euphemism! We talk about "loss" and "losing" people as though they were somehow still around, if only we could find them!) The reality of death and dying is not an agreeable one, for sure, and often profoundly distressing when it affects us personally. We disguise and mystify its awful, magisterial truth by prettifying it with the common euphemisms, along with the contingencies that surround it. People die, and unless you believe—as many do, though I do not—in an alternative existence after death, they don't "pass" or "pass on."

I understand the need. We tiptoe around death in part perhaps because the notion of no longer being a living presence here on earth is intolerable to us. We fear death's imminence, its omnipresence and omnipotence, especially as we age and watch it carelessly snatch our friends and family from us with dreadful and increasing frequency. Not knowing where they go, we say they "pass" because we don't want death to be the end of everything—at least for those of us for whom the notion of rebirth or the resurrection of the physical body is neither intellectually nor emotionally defensible.

Is it cruel to speak directly of "death" and "dying" when we have agreed upon these euphemisms to make their truth more palatable? Surely, it's more honest. I do, however, note my own tendency to engage in circumlocution when I understand that feelings could be hurt. There's no point in being callous. But something in me finds it hard to say utter the word "pass" instead of "die", or "passing over" when what I really mean is death.

I have friends who believe that death is the final curtain. There is no sequel, no replay, no encore. Just nothing. First you live, then you die. I have other friends who like to believe in an afterlife, a heaven, if you will. Or hell. I have still other friends who want to believe there's *something* that survives, a consciousness that persists in one form or another. If put to it, my own preference is to accept that any such speculation on the unknowable is idle. I reject the harsh judgment of atheism just as I reject the bromides of believers. I prefer simple realism. "Let us imagine a number of men in chains," wrote Blaise Pascal, "and all condemned to death, where some are killed each day in the sight of the others, and those who remain see their own fate in that of their fellows and wait their turn, looking at each other sorrowfully and without hope. It is an image of the condition of man." It's an image that I find compelling, inarguable. The rest, as Hamlet said, "is silence."

Chicken Little

For a long while it has seemed clear to me that planet Earth will have a much brighter future once it shrugs off our benighted species, humankind. Or, as the poet e.e.cummings nicely put it, *manunkind*. The thought originated when I was still a teenager, writing feverish adolescent poems of doom inspired by favorite writers like George Orwell, predicting the headlong rush of humanity toward self-destruction, overpowered by the dreaded "machine." Then came Hiroshima, followed by the fifties and the Cold War, and the invention of ever more powerful weapons that could destroy whole cities and, eventually, literally, the entire human species. Following swiftly on the heels of this scenario of entirely plausible nuclear cataclysm came the growing realization among responsible scientists that what in our human arrogance we call "progress" is destroying the habitat on which our lives depend, and doing so with alarming, soon-to-be-irreversible speed.

Then came yet another warning, the coronavirus pandemic and the mass death it brought upon us. And now, as if the harrowing threats of apocalyptic weaponry, wanton destruction of habitat, and virulence of disease were not enough, I learn that we must now add to that list the potential scourge of artificial intelligence. AI. The term has hovered around the periphery of my consciousness for some time, but now I hear and read about it everywhere. Most of us have paid scant attention as it has slipped quietly into every aspect of our lives to become, now, a lurking threat to the future of humanity. It is the stuff of fiction. George Orwell was no fantasist, but prescient. This new means of control is available to anyone who might wish to subjugate us. Hal, the malevolent computer of 2001, has in the 2020s become an imminent threat we must contend with, one that could eject us from the little global spacecraft on which we travel through infinite space without so much as a twinge of human conscience.

I conclude that Chicken Little was not as crack-brained as we were taught to believe as children. The sky is actually falling.

RomCom

The series keeps teasing you with the notion that it's a romantic comedy, then slapping you across the face with not-very-comedic twists and turns. Sometimes playful. Sometimes not. "One Day", a British television production, had Ellie and me on tenterhooks through each of its numerous short episodes.

The "one day" is July 15, St. Swithun's Day—a kind of Groundhog Day in the UK, where local lore predicts:

> *St. Swithun's day if thou dost rain,*
> *For forty days it will remain.*
> *St. Swithun's day if thou be fair,*
> *For forty days 'twill rain nae mair.*

The series follows events in the lives of its main characters, Dexter and Emily, on that one day over some twenty years. The first is the day that boy meets girl: eyes lock across the space of a crowded dance floor on their graduation day at Edinburgh University. They meet, they sleep (almost) together, they climb a mountain, and they part... each caught in a lasting obsession with the other.

The ingredients are mostly romcom. The brief encounters over the years, the misunderstandings and the missed connections, the false starts and poignant endings. The pair are traditional soul mates, fated to be together but frustrated at every turn. Em is a second or third-generation feminist—smart, quick-witted, insistent on her independence, and a wee bit cynical, especially about men. Not exactly pretty in the conventional sense, but lovely, captivating to the eye. Dex is an utterly charming scoundrel, lovable, irresistible to women, spoiled by too much wealth and privilege, dissolute, addicted to sex, drugs and rock 'n' roll, saved from repugnance only by a kind of innocence and longing. In short, the two are opposites in every way. But then there's love. Chemistry. Inexplicable mutual attraction. Passion.

For those who have not already come across this series, I recommend it. I will not be the spoiler, but I can offer the assurance that things will not turn out as the viewer expects them to. There's plenty of fun and no shortage of laugh-out-loud moments, but also a convincing depth of emotion, hurt, and pain. A very appealing drama with all the confusion and vulnerability of real human beings caught up in an imperfect world that always has us wishing things were different and better than they are and yet, if we are wise, content with the measure of happiness we can find.

Our 50th

Few people can have enjoyed so beautiful and strange a 50th wedding anniversary as Ellie and I did yesterday.

The previous year had been a challenging one for Ellie. A person who had always enjoyed the best of health, had always eaten well and taken care of herself with regular exercise, she had been devastated by the unwelcome news of a cancer diagnosis. By the time the date of our 50th anniversary came around (11/11, Armistice Day in England, Veterans Day here) she was well into a prescribed course of chemotherapy. And since the prospective loss of the hair that had always meant so much to her self-image was particularly hard for her to contemplate, she made a brave decision: rather than allow herself to become a victim to the cancer, she chose to disempower the disease by taking things into her own hands. She would make a ritual of the inevitable moment and make it hers.

When the day of our anniversary arrived, some twenty of Ellie's closest women friends came to our home to bear witness—and a few who could not come in person came on Zoom, remotely. I was privileged to be the only male on hand and was reminded, oddly, of another landmark celebration: my 21st birthday, which for reasons I no longer recall was celebrated with my mother, six girls, and myself. But I was happy to be included among so many beautiful and loving "angels", as Ellie rightly calls them.

Many of our guests had no idea it was our anniversary—we had not made a point of it—but were delighted to celebrate the occasion with us once they learned. But we had another, even more important purpose, the ritual that Ellie had planned. As a first step, she went around the circle, identifying and recognizing each of her guests with grace, gratitude, and a needed touch of humor, and addressed each one with a few words of love and appreciation. As she made clear, every one of them had a special and important place in this pantheon, some of them very old friends, some of them quite new.

Once introduced, these good women were invited to witness the main event, the ritual shaving of Ellie's head, her act of defiance against the power of the disease. An awed silence fell upon everyone there at the first sound of the scissors. It was interrupted only by the occasional ambient sounds, soon forgotten and remained unbroken for the length of the entire ritual, a spell none of us would have wanted to break, unless with a few spontaneous gasps of wonder as the scissors gave way to the electric razor and the awesome contour of Ellie's shaven head began to emerge--when the silence was finally broken by a few impulsive muttered comments around the circle: "She's so beautiful!" I heard.

There were tears, too, as I could not help but notice. Sarah's tears, certainly, our daughter's. And my own. For many years I have known how much importance Ellie has attached to her hair and its care, how much it has been a part of her identity, her sense of self. Now she was letting it go. She sat, eyes closed, in total concentration and total serenity. And those of us around her were just simply amazed. When the ritual was over, the sense of elation that we shared was tangible, as was the love that was finally released to overwhelm her. We were all caught up in the great wave of emotion.

Afterward, when we had all calmed down, I read the story of our marriage that I'd written the day before and posted on my Facebook page. It succeeded in lightening things up and readying us all for a glass of champagne. Well, prosecco. But who cared? It tasted great. Ellie and first toasted each other, then everyone joined in. Toasts all around. A sense of joy and community that eventually devolved into the kind of friendly chatter known to partygoers everywhere.

There followed a feast of crackers and assorted cheeses, of various sweets, and a delicious chocolate cake made by Marah, Sarah's oldest friend and the daughter of Ellie's own oldest friend, Kirsten, who joined us on Zoom from San Miguel de Allende. Everyone stayed on, reluctant to leave, and the party went on much longer than planned.

What a day! What a celebration! What an occasion for gratitude, despite the adversity that Ellie faces with such courage and determination. We are fortunate indeed to have such friends, and to have so very much love to share with them.

Adorable

I dreamt I had a tiny tabby kitten, small enough to hold in the palm of my hand. She was called Millie, short for Million Dollar Baby. That's all I can remember.

Insecurity

The dissertation I labored over long and hard at the conclusion of the vast number of years I devoted to what some would consider an excessive education was titled "Magicians of Insecurity." The title was borrowed from an essay about the art of poetry by a noted French poet whose name—my apologies!—I have long since forgotten. *Ars poetica*, the technical term for this literary convention, was the theme of my dissertation. The kind of insecurity this poet referred to was that of humanity at large, *la condition humaine*, in a post-Enlightenment world where belief in the existence of a God, or gods, no longer undergirds the meaning of one's life. In the field of literary drama, the same philosophical reality led to the "Theater of the Absurd".

Not many years after the completion of that dissertation and soon after the great 1971 Sylmar earthquake that convulsed the Los Angeles area, I contributed an essay to one of those ephemeral art magazines that used to pop up on the West Coast from time to time. It was called "Living on a Fault". I had been looking at the work of artists who interested me because they were aiming for something quite different from that old ideal of masterpiece perfection. I was absorbed, too, in the Japanese aesthetic of *wabi-sabi*, which attributes beauty not to perfection but, precisely, to the artwork's flaw; or, as Leonard Cohen sang in his own cracked voice, the crack "where the light gets in."

I have learned to embrace insecurity in the same way I embrace imperfection. It is not only the Buddhist dharma that teaches us to acknowledge the essential truth of the human condition, that we have no way of knowing what will next occur, even from one moment to the next. As illness unkindly reminds us, life is fragile; and while we know that death is inevitable, no one can predict when and how it will arrive. If we are to find happiness, we must learn to live with insecurity.

Beyond the nice abstractions of philosophy and religion, however, and in the real experience of life, I have noticed a growing sense of insecurity in myself and all around me. I see it everywhere. It is impossible to feel secure when fundamental facts are under assault from all quarters, let alone truth itself. So-called "disinformation" is rife, spread almost instantaneously through social media and exploited by those who care more about power than the truth. Blinded by misguided loyalty, millions of my fellow citizens seem ready to act with violence, if necessary, to defend the lies propagated by dangerously weak, self-interested leaders. Even as I write, the election of a demonstrably narcissistic, sociopathic madman seems entirely possible, to lead not only the country but the world into chaos with his delusions of grandeur.

Given this circumstance, I find it impossible to cling to any sense of security; even twenty-five years of meditation practice are inadequate to calm my fears.

On the other hand, in a perverse kind of irony, we Americans share an equally illusory, equally senseless demand for indemnity from all of life's contingencies. The slightest accident or mishap is an offense against everyone's absolute right to protection from adversity, and any perceived infringement on that right, whether by a fellow citizen, a business enterprise, or even the government, is the cause of righteous outrage—and likely, too, a lawsuit. We lack a middle path where we embrace the perhaps unwelcome truth of insecurity. It's up to each of us, of course, if we seek happiness, to find that middle path.

Without a minimal sense of security—or at least the comforting illusion of it—we humans are in a pitiable predicament. I can't help but think, as I write, about those millions of our fellow men, women, and children in Gaza and Ukraine who are under the incessant deadly threat of bombs and shells. For them, security is an unimaginable luxury, to be grasped at best in fleeting moments, as it is for those many millions more throughout the world who are forced into patterns of migration by violence at home, or the ravages of climate change that deprive them of life-giving food and water and leave them at risk of illness, malnutrition, or starvation.

No matter, then, that I feel unsafe in the context of our current political and social melodrama here in America, I try to keep my personal malaise in perspective and remain grateful for the extraordinary good fortune and privilege that I enjoy.

Smile

As an antidote to recent thoughts about insecurity, I found it useful this morning to do a smiling meditation. The best part is that you don't need anything to smile about. After bringing your restful attention to the breath, you simply allow your lips to settle into the shape of a gentle smile. You'll find that the mind soon adapts to the physical shape of the lips, and the smile takes over the whole body. That done, you can simply rest in attention to the smile.

Depression: Part I

I have hesitated long and hard before writing these thoughts down, fearful that they might be misinterpreted as a plea for sympathy. But no, if I put them down on paper, it is rather in the hope of offering a mirror to my fellow travelers through this strange and wonderful and endlessly fascinating world, and to give my personal testimony to the fundamental truth that we are all, in so many essential ways, the same.

So here's the fair warning. Close your eyes it you prefer not to read, your ears if you prefer not to hear. I'm about to record something further about myself that you may not want to be bothered with. I do so as always out of this strange and frankly rather embarrassing compulsion to tell the world what it doesn't need to know about this one of its creatures. (Any reader who feels inclined to know the even more embarrassing truths about me will have to read my fiction, where I feel free to tell the truth in an imaginative guise).

So here it is. I am experiencing—by no means for the first time—a bout of listlessness, disinterest, disengagement, and even alienation that mental health professionals would probably call depression. I dislike labels, but this one has the uncomfortable ring of truth. I am blessed in that I suffer from a relatively mild and ephemeral version of this common malady, but enough to give me a glimpse into the total, unmitigated darkness I know others experience, described with such painful intensity by William Styron in *Darkness Visible*—a book that I read years ago to help me understand the depression of a person close to me; or by the poet John Berryman in the 14th and to my mind, the most brilliant and distressing of his "77 Dream

Songs", the one that starts out with that memorable, funny, forthright, devastating line: "Life, friends, is boring. We must not say so…"

For myself, in the mild version of depression I experience from time to time as age exacts its toll, it takes the form of cruel, irrational attacks on the value of my life and work: I have not been the writer that I could have been; I have not lived up to my potential as a man; I have made unforgivable mistakes along the way; and so on. Perhaps my reader knows this story. It comes down to a sense of worth; or, in this current state of mind, of worthlessness.

I know better now than to try to fight off the depression; the struggle simply serves to dig a deeper hole. Instead, I have learned to acknowledge it and to watch it carefully until, like every other cloud that appears on my horizon, it simply, inevitably drifts away.

Radical Acceptance

The simple truth amply validated by everyday experience is that there are endless sources of suffering in our lives. If we are not vigilant, they take up residence in our minds like unwelcome squatters and refuse to leave. They become our constant preoccupation, our security blanket, and if we're not careful our whole reason for being. So it behooves us to pay attention and not get attached to them. Which is where radical acceptance comes in.

When we identify a source of suffering our first question needs to be: what can I do about it? Let's say it's physical pain, such as I happen to be experiencing in my left hip at this moment. Have I done what I could? Yes, I took my pain to the doctor, who tried two successive cortisone injections. The first one worked for a while, the second one didn't. I took the pain to the orthopedic surgeon who examined the x-rays and recommended surgery. Given the way things are in health care these days, there was a three-month wait before it could be scheduled. What should I do about the pain in the meantime? Pills, the doctor said. I did what I could. I took the pills, but the pain persisted. It would not go away. The only choice left was radical acceptance.

It is not easy, but here's where meditation comes in handy—for me at least. I breathe. I bring my full attention to the breath. Sometimes when I direct the breath to the source of pain, acknowledging its presence and watching it intensely, the pain will slowly dissipate. It's there, then it's not there quite so much anymore, and then it's gone. No way to explain it any better. Alternatively, I redirect my attention from the source of pain to some other place in my body, someplace where I am not experiencing pain, and keep it focused there. Or I decide instead to keep it focused on the breath itself.

The important part is not to deny the pain, nor struggle with it, nor resist it. The important part is to recognize that it is there and accept it for what it is. Pain. The skill is to accept that truth without attaching to it, without identifying with it, without allowing it to become "my pain" and thus define me.

But of course, it is not just physical pain that is the source of suffering. It can just as well be a persistent emotion, fear, or grief, or anger. I can get attached to my anger at someone for something that they did or failed to do. Especially if I am convinced I'm right, that my emotion is justified, I can't let it go. If I'm not vigilant it can take over my life, defining me. My anger becomes who I am. The solution is the same as with physical pain, however. The first question is always: what can I do about it? Can I speak to this person, find common ground, forgiveness? Is there something else I can do to remove the source of anger? No? Then the answer is the same: radical acceptance. It is the same with grief or fear, which can also define me if I let them.

Another major source of suffering for me, as it surely is for others, are my thoughts and judgments. Particularly those judgments. I look out at the world and I see warfare, famine, illness. I see evidence of a changing global climate and millions of the world's inhabitants fleeing the country of their birth to find security elsewhere, frequently in countries that do not welcome them. Here in my own adoptive country, I see disreputable men seizing power and cynical politicians failing to debate the important, pressing problems they were elected by constituents to resolve. I see a judicial system willing to give a free pass to villains and tricksters while good people suffer from injustice, hatred, racial prejudice, neglect. I make judgments about all this. I know them to be sound judgments, arising from the human compassion that I feel. I judge those who fail to share that compassion—and judge myself among the righteous.

All this troubles me, deeply. Again, the first question is this: what can I do? I do what I can. I vote. I make my voice heard, though it seems to me often in the wilderness. I send checks where I think money can be well used, but they are tiny drops in the huge bucket of need. Nothing I do feels like anywhere near enough, and my own suffering intensifies in the face of the powerlessness I feel in the face of forces inestimably greater than those I can muster to address them. Acceptance is required of me if I am not to relinquish my hold on sanity and a modicum of happiness.

No one ever said that radical acceptance is easy. A skill that needs to be honed to a fine edge, it is always a work in progress, never work done. It goes against every natural inclination, every impulse that we must exercise control in our lives and protect ourselves from harm. Even so, it's good to remind myself that acceptance does not entail quiescence. It does not require me to be the doormat for anyone who cares to step on me. As I have been at pains to point out it requires me, first, to do everything I can. And yet when I summon the strength of mind to practice radical acceptance it is the most effective means of solace and respite from what Hamlet called "the slings and arrows of outrageous fortune." These will keep coming at us, no matter what we do, so it's better to be armed and ready with an effective strategy of defense than to become their victim.

For all of this, there is a useful mantra: "This is not me, this is not mine, this is not who I am." Repeat it often enough and you'll begin to actually believe it. You can learn to watch all kinds of pain as though from a remote distance, as though through the lens of a telescope held in reverse, an object to be observed with almost scientific disinterest rather than connection. In this way it becomes more like an abstraction than a reality, and therefore less a source of suffering.

And all it takes is practice, practice, practice.

Peggy

I am thinking this morning of my mother, Peggy, née Margaret Gladys Williams, on whose 30th birthday I was born in 1936. She was a hardy Welsh girl, brought up in her earliest years barefoot, as she recalls it, on the streets of London's East End. Legend has it that the family lived on Pudding Lane, that iconic East End street where the Great Fire of London started in 1666. Peggy's father, my grandfather, "Grimp," was a proud Welshman, the Rev. Maurice H. Llewellyn Williams, at that time a curate in the inner-city parish of Spitalfields. The family later moved to Swansea, where Grimp was the incumbent in the parish church of St. Gabriel's, where they stayed for most of their lives and where Peggy spent her later childhood years. Before his retirement, Grimp was inducted as a Chancellor of Brecon Cathedral, the flagship of the Anglican Church of Wales.

Grimp's wife, my grandmother, Peggy's mother, was an Isaacson by birth, though she always insisted that her family were "the non-Jewish Isaacsons"—in London's Jewish East End! This even though she spoke fluent German and, I believe, a smattering of Yiddish and had in her possession a lovely antique side table inlaid with Hebrew lettering. Still, as the wife of an Anglican minister she could hardly be Jewish, could she? Had she been Jewish, however—which she surely wasn't, heaven forbid—this would have made my mother Jewish by matrilineal descent, and myself, therefore, a Jew. A small and plucky woman, Grane—as she was known in the family—was an Air Raid Warden in the badly bombed Swansea in World War II, where she would alarm her fellow wardens by bringing back wheelbarrows loaded with the unexploded incendiary bombs she collected after the air raids. She kept one of them, disarmed, in her attic, and allowed me to play with it as a child.

Peggy had four siblings. Stephen, the progenitor of a still-thriving Williams line, was the oldest. Then there were three younger sisters: Nina, a frequent visitor to our Rectory during the war and something of a flapper in my childhood memory; she loved her "gin and It"—Italian vermouth, and therefore I suppose, what we would now call a martini. Jocelyn, Jo, like her father, like Peggy, also married an Anglican priest and emigrated with her family to Australia after the war. Then was Gay, Gabrielle, the youngest.

So I was born on Peggy's birthday, a birthday present, as Harry liked to joke. Aside from being mother to myself and my sister, Flora, she was a loyal wife to her husband, a pillar in the church he served and in the village community, and a brilliant keeper of the Rectory household. During the war years, she opened the big house not only to refugees from London but also to *billetees*--service men and women from the RAF and the Royal Navy and three of the brilliant "Bletchley Girls" who worked at the super hush-hush Bletchley Park—one of whom was her own sister, Gay. More of this later. Peggy was also a wonderful cook, a skilled typist and stenographer whenever Harry needed one, and an ardent gardener. She dug potatoes, picked and preserved fruit and berries from our backyard, and supervised the pantry whose shelves, even during the war years, were always amply stocked with jams, stewed fruits and the makings of the cakes she baked so well for us children. She took me and for walks in the countryside and taught me the names of countless birds, and trees, and wildflowers.

It must have been hard for Peggy in later years to see her children, Flora and me, move so far away; and harder still, as a grandmother and a devoted Christian traditionalist at heart, to see us both divorced and to have at least two of her grandchildren grow up far off in America—a country she honestly did not much like when she came to visit here. She died not long after her husband, having moved from their seaside cottage to a home for elderly women where she felt estranged, certainly, but was comforted by the view from her window of her beloved Teifi river valley, where in better times she loved to watch the fishermen launch their coracles—circular basket boats, waterproofed in coats of black tar—to fish for the river's then still bountiful harvest of Welsh salmon.

I was asked just yesterday—perhaps it was this that had me thinking about her—to name the quality I inherited from my mother. I joked, first, about my blue Welsh eyes. But the word that came to me a moment later, the word that rang true, was "loyalty". Her Harry was not an easy husband. For years he suffered from the intestinal pains the family referred to as his "ulcer." I suspect his ailment was more complicated, perhaps more—to use one of his own favorite diagnoses—psychosomatic, a symptom of his life-long struggle as a Christian minister with his faith in God. He was also something of a charmer, something of a flirt. I do not know if he ever acted out on his flirtations, and I never will. I think I also do not wish to know. Peggy stuck by him through all those years, his faithful, unfailing support and helpmate.

So, yes... loyalty. It's in my bones. but in that context, I must make a confession: many years ago, before I was old enough to know better, I was once terribly, hurtfully, destructively disloyal, and my disloyalty was the cause of lasting suffering. I can only claim to have learned from that experience never to repeat it. And I never have.

Harry

Oh yes. Harry was a flirt.

There was Fiona. This was when the war was on. I would have been five or six years old when she came to live in our house, one of the Bletchley girls to whom I alluded earlier. She must have been in her early twenties, and she was the most bewitching other-than-mother, other-than-sister feminine presence in my life. Even now, some eight decades later, she wanders through my dreams and memories on occasion, a warm, languorous, ever-mysterious presence with a smile that at once invites and puts you in your place.

The Bletchley girls worked under the leadership of the belatedly acclaimed Alan Turing and other notables, whose contributions to the success of military action in World War II were so hush-hush they were kept under wraps for decades after the war ended. The Bletchley Park mansion where they worked was only much later revealed to be the location of the now-famous Enigma Machine, captured early in the war from a German submarine and used to decode vital secret orders from the German High Command to troops in the field. Some say this effort was a deciding factor in the Allied victory.

Fiona was among those "billeted" to our house at the time because we had plenty of empty rooms in our big old Rectory, and because our village was conveniently close to Bletchley. I was old enough to know that their work was very important, very secret, and never, ever to be questioned or even mentioned in our home. The girls—Fiona, Vivian and Gay—came and went every day, as I recall, on bicycles. But perhaps I am wrong about that. Perhaps, as I have read in the literature, there was a car that brought them back and forth.

While Fiona would have seemed no more than an especially talented young working woman to my parents and others in the house, but to me she was to me the great, mysterious, unfathomable feminine, a kind of goddess who moved inscrutably through my life with impossible elegance and glamor. Her body was so voluptuous, her breasts, thighs and hips so full and sweet that, as a small boy, I was overwhelmed by her powerful physical allure. I remember most of all the fragrances that accompanied her wherever she would go, the exotic aura of powders and lotions, perfumes and scents. I remember her lipsticks, the intense red colors of them, the way she would shape her mouth to apply them, the way she would rub her lips together to spread the color evenly throughout. I remember her sheer nylon stockings and the shocking spectacle of garters and other intimate garments on the long washing line in our back garden. I was, in a word, enchanted. I was, insofar as a six- or seven-year-old can be, in love.

I remember too, vividly, wide-eyed, the time that all the residents of the Rectory got together for a boisterous evening of melodrama as a distraction from the consuming anxieties of war. Our big living room was converted for the occasion into a makeshift theater, a sheet draped across for a curtain to define the stages. The play was "Murder in the Rectory". The victim, screaming as she died and bloodied with great slashes of lipstick across her throat, was Fiona. The knife-wielding murderer? My father, Harry, the Rector himself.

I was perhaps dimly aware that my rival for Fiona's affections was none other than my father. He must have been some ten or fifteen years Fiona's senior, because I was born on my mother's thirtieth birthday, and he was a year older than she. And no matter his calling as a parish priest, he was not immune to the appeal of women. I have no evidence to suggest that he ever took advantage of his position, his British public schoolboy charm, his Cambridge education, or his rather handsome appearance to succumb to the temptations of the flesh, but Fiona was certainly among them. And my father was certainly no prude: Jung and Freud were guiding lights in the constellation of what were, for an English country priest, some rather up-to-date notions about sex. Throughout his life he responded eagerly to everything of sensual appeal, including food and wine, and it would not surprise me to know that he had fallen for Fiona's unquestionable charms. My mother hinted, later in life, that things had not always been easy in their marriage. It could well be, I have quite reasonably thought, that Fiona was the cause of one of them.

It pains me also to report that my father's indiscretion did not go unnoticed by those responsible for security at Bletchley Park. It was only decades later that I stumbled on a contemporaneous official report about his questionable behavior. "There is a parson in this neighborhood," the report reads in part, "whose name is the Rev. Harry L. Clothier... We have had a number of people billeted there from time to time and as a host he is very kind. He has, however, apparently acquired a good deal of information about Bletchley Park, some of which gets rather close to the knuckle. The girls who are billeted there now are getting a good deal disturbed about him because he not only seems to try and catch them out with the idea of obtaining a little more information, but he repeats what he knows to everyone that comes to the house and seems to take a quite unchristian delight in getting the girls into an awkward position when introducing strangers."

This was of course a profoundly shocking revelation. But did Harry's habit of "getting the girls into an awkward position" include advances, wanted or unwanted, of a licentious nature? I admit to a certain prurient curiosity, but of course I will never really know.

The Windermere Children

I was browsing through a list of movies on one of our streaming sites when I paused at the rather blandly titled "The Windermere Children." I paused because I myself was a Windermere child. Not like the children in this quietly powerful movie. No, I was by comparison a lucky one. I spent an early childhood year in that spectacularly beautiful spot in England's Lake District, Wordsworth country, because my boys' boarding school was evacuated there for the duration of the war years, far from the danger of its exposed south coast location. The vistas of Lake Windermere and the pungent aroma of its lakes and forests with their blankets of decaying leaves are buried in a corner of my consciousness where they will never be forgotten. Sent away from home and separated for the first time from my parents at the age of seven, I associate those memories with great sadness and loneliness, as well as with that awesome natural beauty.

But I was the lucky one. The children remembered in the BBC 2 production arrived there by the busload just a couple of years later. They were Jewish children, teenagers and little ones, mostly Poles, deeply traumatized after their rescue from the camps in Germany where their families had been decimated, their parents snatched away before their eyes and sent off to be slaughtered. As terrified as cornered rabbits, suspicious of kindness to the point of paranoia, they find it almost impossible at first to adjust to their new environment. At their first breakfast, stupefied by the sight of ample bread on their tables, they grab handfuls of it and scurry off to bury scraps wherever they can find a hiding place.

It's a tale of struggle and eventual redemption. Headed up by a gentle German exile, Oscar Friedmann (played by Thomas Kretschmann), the staff have as much to learn about how to care for these children as their wild young charges, who must now learn to readjust to life in a normal, kindly, unthreatening world. So, too, the locals, distrustful of the sudden appearance of these foreigners in their midst and unable to imagine the trauma of their visitors' previous lives. Mistaking them for Germans, the local boys taunt the new arrivals with mocking Nazi salutes and have to be shamed into silence by Friedmann's caring and respectful rebuke. The climactic scene, four months later, when the time has come for the refugee children to leave their temporary safe haven, is a friendly soccer match between the boys from the camps and the boys from the village.

"The Windermere Children" is a celebration of humanity, and compassion, of good people working together to do good things, and of the redemptive power of nature. The film ends in a lakeside reunion of a handful of the surviving boys as old men, some seventy years later, remembering their time at Windermere with quiet gratitude. The texts accompanying their words are offered to show that these few, at least, and hopefully many others, were helped by compassionate fellow humans as they struggled to survive the terror of the camps and move on to successful and rewarding lives.

I could not help but think of Ernst, as I watched this movie. Ernst was a young Austrian boy, a refugee who arrived in England on the "Kindertransport" and lived with us in the Rectory for several years. He later came to America to rejoin the parents from whom he had been separated, and who had earlier converted to Christianity to escape Nazi persecution in their native Vienna. In thanks, they sent CARE packages to us in the post-war years, and we were always thrilled to unpack great tins of ham and huge jars of peanut butter, along with countless other exotic delicacies from the United States. Ernst recognized a debt of gratitude to my parents, particularly Harry, and he became a dedicated Christian. He remained a loyal, lifelong friend to my parents, as well as to my sister Flora and myself.

Like most of his contemporaries, a decade or so older than myself, Ernst is now no longer with us. The number of those of who still have vivid memories of World War II continues to dwindle, but none of us will forget those years. To most, I'm sure, it's a matter of horror and disbelief that even today there are men in power who have learned nothing from that grim century and choose to ignore its lessons for humanity—witness recent tragic, truly horrific events in Gaza and Ukraine. If anything is gained by waging war, in the long view of history, we know that it will soon be lost again. Until we learn that lesson many millions of innocent beings will continue to suffer needlessly and die. And there will be many more war-scarred Windermere children whose wounds, unseen, will need the healing power of love.

Oppenheimer

Speaking of war and movies, Ellie and I went to see *Oppenheimer*. I came away less than impressed.

First, we made the unwise choice to see the film in IMAX format, where the visual bombardment of the senses overcomes any appreciation of the film's content. Hollywood's trailers continue to be obsessed with monster weapons, explosions, massive car crashes, and the one we saw was no exception. It was a prodigious, all-fronts assault on every physical sense as well, of course, as simple common sense. The eyes are overwhelmed with flashing light and color, the ears deafened by explosions. These days, too, even the body trembles in the poor viewer's seat, racked by the impact of exploding bombs and crashing hunks of metal.

Oppenheimer, too, does not stint on the frequent, spectacular iterations of graphic evocations of Trinity, the test explosion of the first atomic bomb. Searing columns of spiraling smoke and flame sear your eyeballs, consuming the entire field of vision as thunderous explosions pitch you in your seat and reverberate inside your eardrums. You are consumed by the "you-were-there" realism of the historic moment. Still, the volume of the IMAX sound system is not restricted to these dramatic moments. Even the sound of regular speech is exaggerated by multiple decibels and registers so loud that the dialogue is hard to follow. Important plot points are swallowed up in the din.

Also hard to digest is the cast of characters. The story is crowded with scientists and politicians of such note that you really wish for the opportunity to recognize and distinguish between them all. Albert Einstein, of course, is unmistakable for his shock of wild white hair. But for a person like myself who is in any case challenged by facial recognition, it becomes impossible to tell Edward Teller from Niels Bohr or Enrico Fermi from Klaus Fuchs—distinctions which are not only important if you want to follow the plot but also of key historical interest. If only these characters had name tags to identify them, or lab coats embroidered with their names! As it was, they merged into a blur, as did the military officials and the opportunistic politicians who, in the years following the war, conspired to destroy the reputation of a man whose work had assured victory only a few years before.

Nicely presented—and with no attempt to oversimplify—was the moral quandary in which Oppenheimer (skillfully portrayed by Cillian Murphy) found himself, as a scientist and a human being, when confronted with the awesome, unbearable consequences of his work. His love life seems to have been as complex and as fraught with moral predicaments as was his partnership with the practical, get-the-job-done military man, General Leslie Groves (a great job by Matt Damon) in leading the Manhattan Project and its often-skittish team of boffins, engineers and technicians to its harrowingly successful conclusion. The moral outrage of antisemitism is also felt throughout, in the context not only of the mass emigration of German scientists escaping Nazi Germany and those who remained, like Werner Heisenberg, who had both the scientific knowledge and the technological skills to create a German atom bomb but were prevented from doing so, ironically, by Hitler's hatred and mistrust of Jews. Antisemitism was also later a significant motivator in the political attacks on Oppenheimer. Having flirted, like so many Jewish intellectuals in the between-the-wars period, with communist ideology and dabbled in socialist organizations he became a prime target for right-wing oppression in a post-war America obsessed with anti-communism. As was also the case with Alan Turing in the UK, a man who served his country with distinction was rewarded with mistrust and castigation.

I wanted to like *Oppenheimer* more than I did. I came away thinking that the history of the development of nuclear weapons and their first use on human populations deserved a more demanding and critical scrutiny than this.

Doctors

I am trying to find words to describe the sensation of standing totally naked, exposing my old man's body to the unsparing gaze of the efficient young woman who stands a couple of feet away from me. Self-conscious? Yes. Embarrassed, certainly. Humbled, exposed, deprived of the usual protections. Surrender of ego and sacrifice of privacy. And is there—surely not?—a barely perceptible sense of excitement? An arousal of the senses, if not the organ? No, not the organ, obviously. Cue the sad music.

Fully clothed herself, my examiner wears a white medical coat and a surgical mask that conceal what I guess, from her dark eyes and long black hair, to be her youth, her beauty, and her vigor. She is my dermatologist. She runs her fingers gently over the blemishes that call for her attention and turns me around to examine the no-more-appealing rear view. Moments ago, I was stretched out on her examination table, my hospital gown discreetly parted to allow her to examine the groin where, last month, she had biopsied a suspicious growth. Poking at the still-sore wound left over from what is delicately called the "procedure," she pronounces herself satisfied with the healing process. However, tucking in the gown on the opposite side to protect my modesty, she finds new cause for concern. Another rash, a different kind this time. I am to apply Vaseline twice daily on one side, she instructs me, and hydrocortisone cream twice daily on the other.

You may laugh. You have my permission. I have to laugh myself. If you can't laugh at the imperfections of the body when you get to my age, you're going to spend the rest of your days in misery.

Just recently I also paid a visit to my podiatrist. Yes, I have one. He dug away cruelly at an ailing big toe with a formidable medical clipper, a more business-like tool than those you can buy in the drugstore and capable of inflicting infinitely more pain. And just last month I was in the office of my orthopedic surgeon—I have one of those, too—to discuss the recovery from my second hip replacement. Next week I will see my ophthalmologist, who will give me another shot in the eyeball to slow the progress of my retinal edema.

This is the story of the aging body. Mine, at least. I spend a great deal of time in doctors' offices, much more than I would like. But I am thankful for the amazing advances in medical care and grateful to those who practice it with such efficiency and compassion. Not many years ago, I remind myself, I would have already been long dead. Yet here I am, alive and still able to kick—though less forcefully than in the past—and happy to have both hips working. Whatever happened, I wonder, to those who suffered from this kind of hip deterioration years ago? They must have accepted life with constant pain. Perhaps we humans were hardier then than now, more resistant, or more tolerant of pain. I'm curious to know, but must add this to the ever-lengthening list of things I never will.

Covid

I am disappointed. Ellie's cell phone rang when we were literally in the car and on our way to a study session on the topic of aging, illness and death. It was to be led by Thanissaro Bhikkhu, abbot of the Thai Forest Monastery and our long-time guide in all things Buddhist. Our daughter Sarah, however, had just stopped by to visit with us after a tour through several European countries with her son Luka and her Dutch friend, Edwin, and now she called to let us know she had tested positive for Covid. We had been looking forward to the mini-retreat—an hour's discussion, followed by a second hour of part-guided, part-silent meditation, but all we could do in the circumstance was stop outside the door at our friend's house and explain our predicament. Having given Sarah and Luka big welcome home hugs just the evening before, we did not want to risk passing the infection on to others, particularly older folk, even though I thought and hoped that the chances of our own infection were minimal. We said a sad remote hello to our friends and, sadly, returned home.

It was a particular disappointment because we had not been able to sit with Than Geoff for many months; and since he himself was late in arriving we could not even greet him with the traditional Thai *wai*, with palms together and a respectful bow. Still, it was at least a pleasure to give our good friends a wave and blow a kiss. Some members of our meditation group have not seen Ellie for some time because of her own health issues and were delighted to catch a glimpse of her. She and I would now have to return to our actual, day-by-day, lived experience of the challenges of illness and aging without the benefit of the Buddhist wisdom we had been looking forward to. We can be thankful that the third topic for the day, death, is not yet in our experience. It still awaits. But we would be foolish not to be aware of its proximity.

I am profoundly grateful to this group of friends. I first stumbled into a tentative meditation practice nearly thirty years ago and would likely not have committed to it quite so deeply had it not been for the love and encouragement with which I was greeted by these good people, as well as the guidance of Than Geoff. Now that I am well acquainted with the aging process and the challenge of illness, I can hardly imagine how it would be to live into still greater age without the measure of equanimity I have learned—along with the humbling realization that there is always more to learn.

It is good to know that I have friends embarked on the same journey as myself, and I am more than grateful for the knowledge that I have a place of refuge where I will always be welcome. I could not ask for more.

Bob Went Home

My friend Gary Lloyd is on the eve of his eightieth birthday, and I am moved to express my love and admiration for a man with whom Ellie and I share a long history of friendship.

I first met Gary in the Orlando Gallery out in the San Fernando Valley —not in person, but through his work. It must have been in 1971. I was a poet at the time, teaching at USC and not long in Southern California—and entirely new to the world of contemporary art. My general knowledge and casual education in art history had taught me about Picasso and Braque and the Surrealists, but very little else, and with this scant knowledge I walked into the gallery expecting to see "art" and instead was shocked by what I found: pages ripped from volumes of "Jane's Fighting Ships"; walls smeared with Vaseline and violently disfigured with a still protruding axe; a row of jars emitting the odor of a mysterious, ill-smelling liquid. And amidst the mess, these enigmatic words scrawled in blue marker on the wall: "When I was a small boy, Bob went home."

I was not only mystified, I was also appalled by this chaos of texts and tasteless, disparate objects that had the effrontery to call itself art. I was so appalled that I was prompted to go home and write a thirty-page poem that I titled "Bob Went Home." The poem was an attempt to come to terms with what I'd seen. It was about little boys making messes, little boys with ink-stained fingers and unkempt hair and dirty clothes; little boys obsessed with their strange bodies and the looming mystery of sex. In other words, the poem was about myself. And about the lived experience that I thought Gary's work was talking about. I wrote and wrote until I could write no more—the first time I had turned my hand to writing about art. I had no way of knowing at the time that the poem was in fact the beginning of a long and rewarding journey, and eventually a whole new professional path as a writer.

Ellie was managing the Art Rental Gallery in the basement of the Los Angeles County Museum of Art back then and it was thanks to her that I met Gary and gave him my poem to read. He was intrigued by what I had written and suggested using it as the text for a "book" that would combine three-dimensional art and words. I happily agreed, and for many weeks thereafter we labored together in his studio to produce an edition of strange, clunky books that we called "Bob Went Home." Its words were printed in IKB (International Klein Blue, after Yves Klein) and its "pages" were constructed of cork sheets, woven cotton pads, roofing materials and even, dangerously, asbestos. Many of them were sheathed in tight wire mesh, legible only by dint of effort and careful manipulation. The "spine" was a hatchet handle and the front cover was a sheet of dented metal.

"Bob Went Home" was the beginning of a long friendship between two little boys who were both still trying to grow up. (Still are!) I have followed Gary's work and have written about it on occasion, notably about his remarkable "Chomsky's Vessel" series with big tomes hollowed out and clamped together in the form of primitive canoes. Like much of Gary's work, they combine profound, often ancient memes and symbols with contemporary technology and sociological critique. Books, the repository of so much human knowledge and history and beautiful objects in themselves, have remained a favorite medium for Gary: Ellie and I treasure a recently completed assemblage of recycled volumes scrawled with a stream-of-consciousness narrative that graces my downstairs study wall.

As have so many of his fellow human beings, Gary has been challenged in his life with turmoil and perhaps more than his share of pain. Throughout, he has maintained a quiet and honorable stoicism, a measure of grace and dignity that sets him apart as a man of integrity as well as a unique and penetrating vision. He has been a "giant" presence in my life, and in Ellie's, and those who know him will recognize this as more than a literary metaphor!

So, these words say Happy 80th, Gary. As I did several years ahead of you, you are entering a noble decade that will continue to bring you the rewards of work and the love of friends. I wish you true happiness now, and in many more years to come.

"My" Ego

As I reflect on the aging process—as the passage of time requires of me so often these days—I have come to understand more clearly how ill my ego serves me. The more I discover ways to leave it behind, the happier I am.

I was thinking about this shortly after waking up this morning, my best time to get focused on the important things before the contingencies of the day impinge on what space remains in the ragged corners of what once I thought of as my brain. Inevitably, it soon gets swamped by a multitude of extraneous, mostly irrelevant thoughts. And thinking about ego, I boiled it down to three major components: *identity, control*, and *ownership*. There are surely others, but I concluded that these three are comprehensive—and each of them illusory.

We think of *identity* as a necessary part of who we are. We expend a good deal of our youthful time and energy in pursuit of answers to that most basic of all questions: Who am I? The arc of time presents us with a variety of practical alternatives, from which we make our choices: tinker, tailor, soldier, sailor, rich man, poor man, beggarman, thief; husband, father, mentor, friend. And so on. We struggle to fit ourselves into the clothes of these characters and wear them to define who in the world we are. At the same time, confusingly, we find it impossible to resist the need to become the person others think we are and seek to live up to the identities they confer on us. We are soon burdened with so many selves! It's hard to keep track of them all, and it takes a huge amount of effort to keep up with them. We suffer needlessly in the attempt.

Old age—and possibly a measure of wisdom—offers a different and more welcome choice: I am nobody. (That lovely Emily Dickenson poem resonates for me: "I am Nobody! Who are you?/Are you – Nobody – too?/Then there's a pair of us!") Having acquired no shortage of identities along the way, I am now happy when I manage to release one. I do better without them. When I shed my identity as "the writer", for example, I'm able write with much greater ease and pleasure, without the suffering that writing used to generate: Is it good enough? Did I say it right? Will readers think me ignorant or stupid? How does it stack up against the work of other, far more accomplished writers? By the same token, when I stop worrying about what it means to be a man, I'm able to slip more easily and confidently into manhood. I need no longer rely on secondhand images of strength and virility to bolster my ego or impress others.

So once I accept the delightful truth of being nobody, I no longer have to prove *I am somebody*. ("How dreary - to be - Somebody!" continues Emily, "How public - like a frog...")

I suffer when I try to impress others with the Somebody I so much want them to see. Old age shows me that the effort is absurd. *Control* is as much an illusion as identity. My ungainly gait makes it obvious that I no longer control the movement of my body as I used to. I hobble along because my left hip hurts. I stumble unpredictably, in danger of a fall. Still more humbling lapses in physical control surely await me, as does dependence on others for the most basic needs. Beyond my own small sphere, I can do nothing to remake the social and political world in accordance with my wisdom. We deceive ourselves with the illusion of control, choosing to ignore the simple truth that the realities of life are indifferent to our wishes and our plans.

If identity and control are illusory, the same is true of *ownership*. We readily succumb to the belief that what we have is *ours*. We even want more. But age comes along to remind us that what we have always thought of as our possessions are never truly ours. The house, for example, that Ellie and I bought many years ago and take for granted to be "ours" belonged to someone else before we owned it and will soon belong to yet another owner. I find it laughable to define myself by the bits and pieces I have accumulated in my life. No matter what my ego likes to think, I am not what I possess, and I only add to my suffering if I surrender to the illusion that I must cling to all this stuff if I want to be the person I imagine myself to be.

To release myself from identity, control and ownership is to discover the freedom that old age can deliver. We understand finally that to continue to attach stubbornly to the fragile illusion of our many egos is to court suffering and dread. To be somebody requires more time, commitment and effort than I have to spare.

Much better to be nobody. If I can.

Alter Ego

I have a friend, another Peter, who likes to mock me in public comments on my social media posts. Let's call him imaginary, for purposes of this discussion, but we could even call this person... my own self since he even shares my name. Call him my alter ego, because he often tells me things I tell myself. He is a person I genuinely admire and like, a man of undoubted integrity and intellect, and he takes me to task for a variety of offenses: for writing too much about myself, for my frequent, lamentable lapses in logic, for my oversimplifications... but most of all for my appeal to matters of the heart and what he sees as my overly easy armchair philosophy, my belief that there are forces at work in the human experience that refuse to be reduced to rational explanation—phenomena he derides in terms like *woo-woo* or *ooga-booga*, but which others call "spiritual". He accuses me, sometimes rightly, of lazy thinking. In short, he holds my feet to the fire.

He is right to do so. I welcome his jibes because they invite me to think again, to question my own assumptions, to dig deeper. At the same time, I often disagree with him (or otherwise myself!) It distresses me when he belittles beliefs that mean so much to others (or myself). There is a smug intellectual arrogance behind the assertion (I'm looking at you, Dawkins, Hitchens, et al.) that all religious thought is bunk, no matter the centuries-old, profound, and continuing debate between men and women of all creeds and races, equipped with far greater intellectual credentials than my own.

My friend also decries my use of social media as a forum for my errant thoughts, as though the practice could substitute for the more laudable act of publication. He is right again. There is no peer review on social media, no professional standard to be met before I put my thoughts out into the world, no critical appraisal after the fact. I write with the clear understanding that those who choose to read anything I write are pre-disposed to agree with it—and indeed to pat me on the back for confirming the opinions that we share (another word of which I can be sure my friend will disapprove!)

I have another old friend from a very different walk of life who inspired me with his concept of the "sacred lifeboat". It's a term that resonates because I sense the need for a place of refuge in a world that increasingly disturbs and alienates me. It pleases me to have the support and love of friends, even virtual ones, and for me the experience of connection is in itself sacred—to resort to another term my good friend will deride. I need, I think we all need, a space where we can agree, a space that is life-affirming and fulfilling, where those of like mind can work together with common intention toward common goals.

There is, too, I admit, the rather puerile temptation to hold the mirror up to my friend, inviting him to consider the thought that in mocking me he might be projecting some of his own intellectual limitations and fallacies. But no—or, as my friend would put it, "nah"—why would I do such a thing? It's better, always, to listen and learn from disagreement; we should all be grateful to have such a friend to keep us honest.

Art Saturday

Yesterday we treated ourselves to a rare afternoon and evening out—an art exhibition, an early movie, dinner. The trifecta. With the incursion of the coronavirus into our lives we began to be cautious about close-quarter public events, especially concert halls and movie theaters, and for a while, we especially missed our Disney Hall concert series. We are happy to feel less constrained these days.

So we stopped by to see the opening of "Garden Spirits", our friend Joanne Julian's show at Tufenkian Fine Arts in Glendale. Joanna is one of those artists whose sheer mastery of her medium makes it look easy. It's not. It's sheer mastery. She is also a master gardener, and her focus in this exhibition is the plants she cultivates with love, the blossoms of flowers and trees rendered with beautiful precision in color pencil and pastel. These are not botanical illustrations, though. Far from it, each one is a love poem to its subject, lyrical, reminding us of the fragility of life itself, catching the passage of a moment in time. The artist leaves ample areas of white or dark space around her subjects—the paper she uses has its own quiet beauty—and for me that empty space is the equivalent of the silence that I love, an invitation to pause and rest in attention, to breathe, in quiet communion with... not nature. That's something different. But with nature seen through another's eyes, seized from its impermanent state and given new timeless life in the form of art. I came away enriched and filled with gratitude.

It did feel good to be back to the patterns of our pre-Covid lives, to be in the company of our fellow human beings, maskless, and without fear of contagion. It felt good simply to see faces, to stand in this beautiful, serene gallery space surrounded by people who share our love of art and chat with close friends whom we have not seen in far too long. It felt like a breath of too-long polluted air...

Virtue

It's a bit old-fashioned perhaps, but I have been thinking about virtue. If the word sounds quaint today, it's because the practice of this quality is little understood or valued at a time when personal comfort and convenience are taken for the prerequisites of the good life, along with financial security, the right possessions, a respected profession or career, and success in life's endeavors. The Stoicism of ancient Greece and Rome—misunderstood these days as little more than the "stiff upper lip"—held rather that virtue was a blend of four essential elements: wisdom, courage, moderation and justice.

The well-known serenity prayer defines wisdom well enough, though I would be inclined to omit the invocation to God. Wisdom, in this prayer, is the resolve "to accept the things I cannot change, the courage to change the things I can, and the discrimination to know the difference." Courage, in my lexicon, is the ability and determination to confront adversity of any kind, whether physical, emotional, or intellectual. Moderation is the Buddhist Middle Path, preventing me from excess to left or right and keeping me in a judicious balance. And justice is the golden rule: respecting the rights and well-being of others no less than my own.

Michel de Montaigne, the French essayist and one of my personal literary heroes, was a great admirer of the Stoics, but his admiration was tempered by a natural skepticism. Theirs were fine goals, he thought, but rarely attainable by fallible, capricious human beings. He refrained from claiming virtue for himself but was surely erring on the side of modesty.

What he shared with the Stoics was a commitment to learn how to lead a worthy life, by which he meant not financial security, not personal success, not comfort, but a life dedicated to the pursuit of fulfillment and happiness for himself as well as others. In this, he shares the guiding principle of the Buddhist dharma, the one that draws me to the practice: what we need if we wish to be truly happy is to find and follow a good way to live—and a good way to die. Which is what I understand by "virtue."

I Googled the fine old French word, *vertu*, a favorite in my lexicon, and came upon a welter of entries touting a luxury brand of cell phone along with referrals to discussions of its benefits versus its cost. I believe my friend Michel, were he to have Google at his fingertips, would simply smile…

Change

Sometimes, when I meditate, I struggle. This morning, the time passed swiftly as I reflected on observing and accepting change. I watched each breath carefully, this new one different from the one before. The next breath too, not the same. Never the same breath twice. I took care to identify the differences between them, some striking, some more subtle, some barely discernable. I used the breath to be comfortable with each and with their difference. In the same way the body, too, never felt quite the same from breath to breath. Watching quietly with interest but without attachment, I became aware of physical differences in the body between today and yesterday, the shifting aches and pains. Breathing, I was able to get comfortable with even those. Here, in this spot a little better from before; over there, a little worse. I was comfortable in the knowledge that in the very next breath there would be a new change to note, to accommodate.

Focusing on changes in the body, I found myself starting to re-experience how it felt when it was newly born, the baby body, and breathed into that phase of existence, rediscovering how it felt to live inside that body. I moved on to the body of the little child, growing through months and years, observing as closely as I could the process of each change, the little chubby legs, the arms, the hands and fingers learning new skills; and the body of the full-grown child, ten years of age, at twelve. Reliving through the remarkable, disturbing changes of the adolescent years, the body continues to grow, growing tall, growing strong, growing into sexual maturity, adulthood. Soon I fell into the pleasant flow of natural physical change, observing, accommodating that process with the breath as I moved on through the years of early adulthood to middle age, and old age, with its current aches and pains. Not yet finished, I moved still further, on into the future, imagining the exact moments before death, the body surrendering, the mind accommodating, the breath accepting each manifestation of change.

At one moment as I watched, my mind appeared to leave the body, expanding into awareness of unceasing change around me. I turned my attention to the sound of water breaking the surface of the pond in the Buddha garden outside my bedroom window, the sound of ceaseless change, of water in constant motion, falling, so that even the body of water in the pond was never still but changed, moment to moment, never quite the same. I attuned my ear to the sound of change, listening attentively, watching, with nothing ever quite the same as in the previous instant, nor in the next. I watched myself constantly accommodating, heedful, resting in attention…

Sometimes, when I sit, I struggle. Sometimes not.

Democracy at Risk

I have been privileged to live in a time when democracy has for the most part thrived, its survival earned by the blood of millions in the course of two world wars. I have known freedom. This was my good fortune. I could have lived at any other time in human history, under kings, dictators, tyrants of all kinds. But no, I have lived for all my life thus far in a democracy, much of it in a country that for all its flaws has been the exemplar of freedom to the world, the goal of every immigrant—like myself. When put to the test by its own flaws, beset by naysayers and misguided people of ill will, this country has always struggled to live up to its original promise. While there is forever more work to do, there has always been a predominant will to struggle toward that "more perfect union."

Now, however, as I approach the last years of my life, I watch in dismay as this democracy is threatened by a wrongfully empowered, would-be authoritarian, who seeks to pervert the history of the country and trample on the rights of its citizens. Looking around me and following media reports from a variety of sources, I find little reassurance in the hope that they will not succeed. Dire times, indeed.

I'm sure I've said this before, or if I haven't I have written around the edges of my conviction that the rise of far-right extremism, whether here in America, in Europe, or in other parts of the world, is driven largely by two related factors: the increasing number of human beings on this planet, this year rising to over 8 billion, and the resultant change in global climate that is driving people from their native countries in search of a better, or merely livable life in less vulnerable areas of the world. Here in America, the immigration stream comes largely—but not exclusively—from countries to the south, from Central and Latin America. In Europe it's the same northward drift, but from northern and sub-Saharan Africa. In both cases, we are witness to an appalling rise in xenophobia.

It was racial hatred of a different kind that drove the malicious nationalist movements of the 1930s. In Europe, it was directed primarily at Jews, a conveniently familiar target of hatred and distrust from centuries past. It appealed to disaffected native populations much as the neo-nationalist rhetoric of today, pointing to some "other" as responsible for the financial woes and social instability that followed the Great Depression. In America, the hatred was directed at the descendants of the slaves on whose backs the nation's wealth was built.

The appeal of extreme right-wing nationalism draws its strength from two powerful human emotions, fear and anger, which are ripe for exploitation by the kind of rhetoric that manipulates its intended targets for political gain. Reason is powerless in the face of its blunt, brutish force. No matter how vile, how loud, how greedy, how unprincipled, and how flagrantly self-interested the leaders of these movements may be, they wield huge power over those they deceive with false promises and lies.

The nationalist propaganda machine in this country is now subordinated to the control of our would-be autocrat, abetted by political enablers cowed into obedience by his narcissistic rage and his compulsion to wrest America from its democratic path and subdue it to his utterly unprincipled will. His vision of a "Great America" is a deeply disturbing reminder of the "thousand-year Reich." Elsewhere, right-wing nationalist clones and aspirants are gaining power around the world, from Italy, Spain and Germany—countries that should have learned better from their own bitter history—to Israel, for God's sake! In Turkey and Hungary as well as more surprisingly in northern European countries, not to mention poor, benighted Russia, there are increasingly powerful nationalist movements; the whole world seems to be teetering on the edge of a frightening authoritarian cliff. The plunge from there is unimaginable.

As of this writing, the battle between democracy and authoritarianism is unresolved in America. It remains to be seen, in the coming national elections, which of the two Americans will choose.

Democrats!

At the risk of incurring the scorn of less tolerant friends, who have been sending out worrisome signals of increasing frustration and revolt in this time of political and cultural hostilities, I need to make my own position clear. This is no time for liberal-minded people like myself to be throwing up our hands and fulminating against those who fail to agree one hundred percent with everything we demand. (Do we need a new term for "liberal," by the way? Too milquetoast-y? The more truculent "Progressive" doesn't quite do it for me either. It's a pity that "socialist" has long since become a dirty word on this side of the Atlantic because I always thought of myself as such. It's a good fit for people like Bernie Sanders and the redoubtable Elizabeth Warren, but none dare call it by its name).

But fellow Democrats are too easy a target and entirely the wrong one.

I hear complaints—and I'm sympathetic—that Democrats are weak-knee 'ed, that they refuse to repulse the ruthlessness of Republicans with their own. But to be ruthless is by definition to be autocratic and thus by definition the very opposite of democratic. I hear it said repeatedly that even when Democrats "controlled" all three branches of government—the House, the Senate, the White House, the Republicans outmatched them. So why can't they get things done, the things we deem important, indispensable? End the filibuster, for example? Expand the Supreme Court and stack it with their own appointments? Abolish money in politics, put an end to gerrymandering, and repeal the Electoral College?

According to this view, the Democrats are a bunch of lily-livered incompetents, so why bother supporting them? The problem, as I see it, is not that their agenda fails to address our multiple problems as a nation, but simply that there aren't enough of them in Congress to effect the needed change. The challenge is not to endlessly complain about their inability to get things done but to elect more of them. Their current minority in the House allows no serious action there. The nearly even split in the Senate might be workable if not for a) the filibuster and b) implacable Republican partisanship. In the face of this, the President is easily caricatured as weak and ineffectual, no matter that by all reasonable standards he has done a remarkable job in maintaining a steady hand in addressing multiple crises, both foreign and domestic.

So it seems to me dangerously disingenuous to keep parroting the simplistic mantra that serves only the opposition, that Biden and the Democrats are weak and powerless and therefore do not deserve the votes of righteous liberals and progressives. The only practical, practicable remedy is not to disparage or abandon those who most nearly represent our views and interests—and, yes, they are less than perfect matches for my own—but to *elect more of them*. Once we have a clear majority in both the House and Senate and are still achieving none of our goals, I'll side with the complainers. But not before. Until that time, I plan to keep doing everything within my own limited power to see do-nothing, obstructionist Republicans booted out, and Democrats elected.

(Note: The above was written before the July 2024 crisis of confidence in the President that for a while created chaos in the Democratic Party and dangerously threatened the path to his re-election in November—a crisis that has been resolved with the withdrawal of President Biden and the spectacular rise of Kamala Harris).

A Commonsense Manifesto

I am no political philosopher or scientist, nor am I a historian. I am simply a man who endeavors to see things as they are and speak honestly. I claim nothing more than plain commonsense and a commitment to human decency as my guide.

And commonsense tells me that when one clearly depraved, greedy, delusional, corrupt, self-interested, and pathologically narcissistic leader can so command the loyalty of a ruthless, subversive minority of political allies, authoritarianism and tyranny are not far behind;

commonsense tells me that uncritical minds are eager hosts for the kind of propaganda that can be readily promulgated by the abuse of both manipulative political commercials and the quagmire of social media;

commonsense tells me that the generational persistence of an underclass of poor and underprivileged people of color is evidence of institutional racism;

commonsense tells me that when a justice system consistently excuses or condones the wealthy and the privileged and condemns those who can ill afford to buy favorable outcomes, that system is a mockery of justice;

commonsense tells me that when politicians are daily obligated to curry the favor of wealthy donors in order to ensure their re-election, they will serve the interests of the wealthy even at the expense of their constituents;

commonsense tells me that in politics as in social justice money talks, and that profits are the guiding principle of a patently unjust and unworkable social and political system;

commonsense tells me that a two-party system of government works only when each party acts in good faith; and that in our current predicament, the one that is acting in good faith is consistently subverted by the other, that is not;

commonsense tells me that the country that was intended as a democracy at its birth has devolved into what can now only be described as an oligarchy or plutocracy;

commonsense requires me to note the gaping discrepancy between what the majority of our citizens say they want, and the policies promoted and enacted by their government;

commonsense tells me that a grotesquely over-armed and increasingly angry citizenry cannot be relied upon to settle differences peaceably;

commonsense tells me that, given the corruption of the electoral system, the gerrymandering of congressional districts, the disproportional representation of this country's voters in the U.S. Senate, the anachronistic Electoral College, the dominating role of money as a political tool, and the adamant resistance to change on the part of one of the two political parties, the prospect of changing the system with the system's self-created tools has become bleak if not unthinkable.

So commonsense tells me that the only salvation for what is left of American democracy must come at the ballot box; that somehow vast, insurmountable numbers of decent, fair-minded, conscientious citizens (and yes, I still believe them to be a majority) must be persuaded to turn out in the next election, before it is too late and despite all obstacles placed in their way, and to abandon old habits of petty self-interest, ideology and party affiliation and instead vote for a candidate, any candidate, who has the courage to embrace simple human decency, plain sanity, fairness and, yes, commonsense.

Cri De Coeur

Enough! Republican leaders must finally admit that their presidential nominee is irremediably compromised and unfit to set foot in the Oval Office for a second time. He has proved himself to be morally deficient and ethically challenged, a congenital and compulsive liar, an arrogant bully, with an ego so fragile it bursts out in childish fits of rage at the least provocation. He has shown himself to be shallow and willfully, proudly, shamefully ignorant. He was first elected in 2016 not with the mandate that he claimed, but rather by a historical minority of American voters—and with the connivance of a hostile foreign power.

Republican leadership must stop claiming to act as though they were doing so in the interest of this country and its citizens. No more attempts to gut a health bill that has saved many American lives and spared millions more the insecurity of living without simple health insurance. No more trashing of international climate agreements to save the planet from the disastrous consequences of man-made global warming. No more backing out of responsibility for leadership among the world's democracies. No more shredding of sensible regulations that protect the environment from exploitation and citizens from corporate rapacity.

Enough! We must call on Republicans to acknowledge the truth that is evident to most Americans. Before they elect their candidate and act upon his proposed agenda to entitle him to the rights of a dictator, they should listen carefully and pay heed to the priorities and preferences of the people they were elected to serve. Their obstinate tone-deafness to what Americans want is reprehensible beyond words.

Enough, Republicans! Enough!

Alas, as the familiar phrase has it: fat chance.

Why?

Why do I do it? Why do I choose to share stories and thoughts that are sometimes so personal in the public forum of social media? It's a question that has been tossed at me from a number of different directions in recent days—and not exclusively on social media. It's a question I often ask myself.

The simple answer, as I've said before, is that it's what I'm given to do. I love that construction, one that I have always thought I borrowed from Robert Creeley—though I have not been able to relocate it. Perhaps it was not in something that he wrote. Perhaps it was something I once heard him say, in my teaching days, when he came to speak and read in one of my classes, and the words stuck.

"What I am given to do." Call it a mission. A mission of service. You may think it fanciful, but I believe we all have a reason for our time here on Earth. A purpose.

It's not because I feel special in some way, especially skilled or gifted, especially wise, or knowledgeable, or compassionate. Not at all. Quite the opposite. It's because I'm convinced that I share a commonality with others, that there is something in my experience as a human being that I share with every other human being. Not everything, obviously. I am unique in many ways, not least in my physical appearance. But there is a vital part of me, I believe, that is shared by every other human being.

I don't know what to call it. Call it heart. Call it mind. Call it collective consciousness. I think of it as the irreducible core of being human that lives somewhere in the relationship between self and other, the bridge we need to cross as best we can in order to persist in our daily lives. Call it connection. It is that which I have wanted to explore in everything I've ever written. Even at those times in my life when I was writing "art reviews" for publication in national magazines, it was the connection I felt driven to explore, the connection between the person who made the art and the person looking at it. I refused to be a "critic" in the sense of one whose responsibility is to distinguish between good and bad and pass on that judgment. The greatest compliment I could receive was something like: "You really got me." Or "You really heard me."

In the sense that I was writing about connection, then, myself was a necessary part of that connection—the other end of the bridge, so to speak, the receiving end. What I do now, having stepped away from my professional life as a writer, is much the same, but—to stick with the analogy—I do it from the giving end of the bridge. I started out as a poet, and I think that this is what poets do. They give out of themselves. They reach in first, then they reach out and touch. It's what Creeley did in "For Love." I write in prose these days, but in some strange way what I write feels more like poetry. It's from the heart.

Autotherapy, one questioner asks? Am I trying to heal my wounds by showing them to the world? Perhaps that's a part of it. I feel unburdened when I know that I have said it right. But I'm also trying to come to an understanding of what I see when I look out at the world, and then to communicate it with words that resonate with others. I want to reach out and "touch" them in a way that just feels human and feels right. It's the same as when I look at a painting and just say, Yes! with all my heart and mind. No questions. No doubts. Just Yes! With an unapologetic capital letter and an exclamation mark. Yes!

So am I trying to make an example of myself, to be the model of humanity? No. I see myself as merely on my mission as a writer, doing what I'm given to do and getting in touch with my fellow human beings. In doing so, I am trying to discover more about what it means to be a human being and, just perhaps, in the process, to become a better one.

The Getty

There is no better way to celebrate one's *eighty-somethingth* birthday than a jaunt with beloved family to the Getty Villa. I know about this. We went there last year, Ellie and I, with our daughter Sarah and her boyfriend from the Netherlands and her rambunctious 10-year-old son, Luka, whose company was a joyful birthday reminder of the passage of my own dwindling years. We went there again just recently, with our grandson from England and his girlfriend. (Joe is just now—laudably, in a world that too often complacently forgets its past! —completing his master's degree in classical studies with a dissertation on ancient architecture, so the model for the Getty villa is well known to him).

It occurred to me once again, as we walked up the hill from the parking garage, that there are judgments to be set aside if one is to be open to the pure pleasure of this place—judgments having to do with unimaginable wealth and how it was acquired; judgments, based on little more than rumor, reputation and news reports, about the character of the man who amassed that wealth; and judgments about its deployment to plunder the cultural heritage of distant lands...

So yes, these thoughts cropped up again, reflections on the deplorably rapacious nature of humanity, the moment I set foot in the current exhibition—a collection of ancient Egyptian artifacts, whose opulence was further testimony to the truth that outrageous wealth can buy you whatever extravagance you please, no less in the ancient world than in today's. In other galleries there was also the disturbing reminder that violence, war and plunder were no less rife in those early days of history than they are today; and that even then men—yes, alas, mostly men—were capable of acts of unimaginable cruelty, as depicted in vivid battle scenes replete with disembowelments, impalements, beheadings. Worse almost, while not committing such acts of terror on their fellow humans, these ancients were inflicting them in the hunt, for sport, on beautiful animals.

All of which need to be duly noted. But then there is art. Awed by everything I saw, I kept wondering—and I realize this is by no means original speculation—how those two starkly contradictory impulses can coexist in the human mind: wanton destruction, and the creation of objects of such beauty. But there it is, they do. And to walk through the Getty Villa is to be reminded at every turn of the artist's obsessive need to get it exactly right, every detail, unsparing of skill and effort. You have only to look down at the patterned tiles on the marble floors. The floors! And then in the paintings on the walls each leaf, it would seem, is evoked with love and care—the same that is lavished, in the gardens, on rows of immaculately tended plants and trees.

I wandered through the galleries, amazed by what those ancient artists achieved. The detail—passionate, sometimes explicitly sexual, sometimes gently humorous—of ordinary human interaction represented on the painted surfaces of those Grecian vases is astounding. I can, as they say, relate. I have been there, in the stories that they tell, as fresh and true today as they were centuries ago. The human faces on those statues carved in hard, ungiving stone continue to speak eloquently today of character and passing mood. The gestures and postures of those sculptured figures, even the ones left limbless by the passage of time, still manage to convey their own peculiar body language with profoundly moving power. Is it not extraordinary, for example, that a male torso deprived of his genitalia—whether by prurient vandalism or the ravages of time—can exude the pride, the aggressive physical strength, the pure sexual spunk of masculinity?

Revisiting all of this, I realized how deeply I love art and not just the "contemporary" version with which I was professionally engaged for many years, and where so much ego is involved. These days, I find myself more than ever moved, as I age, by these creations of anonymous ancients, testimony to the timeless, profound, and ultimately noble striving of the human spirit and at the same time a humbling reminder of my own mortality.

On my birthday, then, I have so much to be thankful for, so much learned, so much re-learned. And so much love in the experience shared with family, and the occasional glimpse of my youngest grandson, his restless energy and impatience stilled for a moment in the presence of an object of pure beauty.

Poor Me

I have been trying to use my meditation practice to address a particular personal flaw that I have been struggling with for years: the deep well of anger that roils in the pit of my belly and occasionally erupts, most especially when I am burdened with some unwanted task, no matter how insignificant. I usually try to hide the anger, both from myself and its unfortunate recipient. I am not always successful, however, and whether I succeed or not, it is inevitably the source of suffering.

I have given much thought over the years to the source of this anger and understand that originates in an old wound, or a complication of various wounds that date from childhood. Yet here I am, now well into my ninth decade here on earth, and still protective of this vulnerable hidden place, and still resentful when it feels invaded. I understand what it means when professionals in therapy speak of healthy boundaries and the importance of maintaining them. Knowing that they exist, however, is not the same as knowing how to manage them, and on this front, I still have much to learn.

I know now that the anger surges when I feel invaded or put upon by others, when my ingrained, compulsive need to be the "gentleman" feels exploited. I was well instructed in that obligation as a child: I learned to be unfailingly polite, accommodating, and considerate of others. I must never risk incurring their displeasure and always put their needs before my own. To this day, I am constitutionally unable to walk through a door in front of anyone, man, woman, or child. You might think my advanced years would leave me feeling entitled to a certain privilege and respect; but no, I stand back deferentially and hold the door until I'm sure that everyone has gone ahead.

That early lesson persists despite the *metta* practice with which I start my meditation every day. *Metta* is loving kindness, the first of the four *Brahma Viharas* in Buddhist dharma. (The other three are compassion, sympathetic joy, and equanimity). The first words of the *metta* practice are "May *I* be happy, may *I* be free from stress and pain…", reminding me of the need to be right with my own sense of well-being before sending the same wishes out to others—family, friends, people we know well and those we don't know at all. Even people we don't like. It might seem selfish at first glance to think of myself first (and Buddha forbid this "gentleman" should be selfish!) but I have come to accept it as a first and necessary step in sharing the wish with my fellow beings. It's impossible, the teaching goes, to send out genuine goodwill to others if I don't feel it for myself.

It took me some time, too, before I could wish for happiness because I was so conditioned by the mundane, trivial connotations of that word. Happiness, I have come to understand, is something other than getting what I want, whether love, or wealth, or the possession of material goods, whether comfort, or success, or recognition, or even the absence of pain. Instead, the happiness wished for in the *metta* practice, "real happiness", is freedom from all that, and knowing how to find it. We find this kind of happiness once we accept the truth that its opposite, unhappiness, is caused by *attachment* to getting what we want; that suffering is not caused by the pain that we experience, which is inevitable in the course of human life, but by being unable to let go of it when it occurs. It is only if we allow it to become the focus of our attention that it turns from pain to suffering. Happiness, understood in this way is no more than the art—the skill—of letting go.

Alas, as with so many other seemingly simple and self-evident truths, the theory is a whole lot easier than the practice.

Prayer

It's Sunday today, the day when every week as a child I would go to church. I would sit on one side of my mother in the Rector's pew, my sister Flora on the other, with all around us my father's congregation and my father himself up by the altar, leading the service, or standing at the lectern to read from the Bible, or standing high up above us in the pulpit to deliver his weekly sermon.

This memory goes back eighty years.

I do not go to church these days. Unless as a tourist, I have not set foot inside a church in all these many years.

I don't pray. When we were little, my sister and I would get down on our knees every night at bedtime, bring our hands together as we were taught, and say our prayers. I don't know what we prayed for. For Mummy and Daddy, surely. And, since this was during the war, for the men and women—it was mostly men, in those days, doing the fighting and dying—whose lives were at risk on the battlefield, in the air, or on the ocean.

I have the vague memory of praying especially for the sailors; we were an island nation, after all, and our navy had for centuries been our bulwark against the French and the Spaniards who kept trying to invade us. This was the time when the Battle of the Atlantic was raging and the German "Wolf Pack" of U-boats still had free range of the ocean between England and America, our main source of supplies of food and weapons of war. Millions of tons of vital freight were being sent to the bottom of the ocean, and many thousands of lives lost to these elusive menaces, until their codes began to be broken by our genius team at Bletchley Park, and the danger was reduced. So, I do remember praying for the merchantmen and for the brave navy sailors sent out to protect them. I remember the powerfully moving hymn we used to sing in church, my mother's favorite:

> *Eternal Father, strong to save,*
> *whose arm does bind the restless wave...*

And whose last lines, memorably, were:

> *Oh hear us when we cry to Thee*
> *For those in peril on the sea.*

My heart constricts even today when I play that melody back in memory.

At my first boarding school, too, we were required to pray, two dozen boys in a dormitory, all kneeling down beside their beds in striped pajamas. At both my boarding schools, indeed, attendance at chapel services was obligatory, though I suspect that by the time I was a teenager, I was already no longer actually praying when I was on my knees. My mind was mostly occupied with more important things—most notably that irresistible thing between my legs, a matter of vastly greater appeal, I confess, than Jesus. But for all those years at school, I went through the formalities of prayer.

I stopped pretending as soon as I left school and have not prayed since. For most of my adult life, it did not concern me; indeed, I gave little thought to the spiritual dimension of my life unless to scoff at what I saw to be the rank absurdity of it. (For these same years I was also unaware that I had a heart, except for the necessary business of pumping blood; that's another, but related, story). Still, those early years must have left their impression on me because there came a time, in my later middle years, when I realized that there was a gaping hole in my life where this part of me had once been. Having long since abandoned Christianity and the belief in salvation, heaven and hell, God, and so forth, I found a more gratifying and acceptable for my "spiritual" yearnings (I put the word in quotation marks because I don't like it; it has largely lost its meaning through the obfuscation of sentimental overuse. But where is the alternative?) I found it, of course, in the Buddhist dharma—the most practical of all guides to the pursuit of a decent, responsible life—and the daily practice of meditation.

Which brings me back to the question I started out intending to address: is meditation, in particular the *metta* practice, another form of prayer?

I have often wondered about this. Both require the same private, quiet, dedicated time. Both allow us to focus the mind and determine what we might need to change or improve in the way we lead our lives. Or our place in the world at large. I can send goodwill to others, as I prayed for Mummy and Daddy, sailors in peril on the sea, world peace. But prayer, it seems to me, presupposes a belief in Someone (or Something?) to pray *to*, as well as the hope for a response—an answer to my prayers. I do not subscribe to that belief. I do not believe that Anyone is out there, ready to take a personal interest in my affairs, still less to intervene. No "Eternal Father, strong to save", no one to "hear us, when we cry to Thee." I see no evidence for anyone "watching over us" and monitoring the affairs of us foolish human beings. While I have no disrespect for those who do, I see no "Higher Power."

So, with no One to pray *to*, I have no reason to pray. But I do meditate. In meditation, I have nothing to ask for and no one to ask for it. When I start out every morning, as I do, with the words of *metta*, "May I be happy, may I be free from stress and pain...", I do not think of this as a prayer for help. The work is mine. I need to find those things within myself. The Buddha is not a god, but rather a human being who found a way to achieve happiness and was gracious enough to show anyone who cares to pay heed and do the work how to do the same. When I wish happiness for myself and others, it is not in the expectation that someone will reach out and solve my problems for me; it is rather that we recognize and choose to follow the path that can make it happen. If there is something that I want or need, even if it's something as big and unattainable as world peace, I can set that as an intention in my mind. It then becomes my own responsibility to bring the intention to fruition in the best way I can, even if only in the small ways that are within my power. I can work to create the peace I'm looking for in my own heart and mind and find ways to share it with my fellow human beings.

So meditation, as I see it, is not just a quiet swath of time devoted to pleading for salvation, forgiveness, wisdom, or even just serenity. It's work. Inner work, but still work. And I don't expect anyone to do it for me. Perhaps a Christian, perhaps even my father (I suspect he might) would argue that prayer is not so very different. That we are each responsible for our own lives, our own happiness, our own salvation.

But then there is God. Who, as I see it, is The Problem.

The Lost Art

There are plenty of dreadful things to say about social media—the triviality, the assault on privacy, the license to broadcast misinformation and outright lies, the vulnerability of users to commercial or political exploitation, and the calumny and vicious personal attacks it can enable. All of these have an element of truth. And yet, as a writer, I have learned to appreciate one thing about it: the ability to start a conversation. When I post something I have written, there are so many different and interesting takes on the topics that I raise, topics that have meaning for me or else I would not raise them.

The act of writing reflects a choice for isolation. It's something I must do alone, and what I write exists often only in an echo chamber. Anyone who dedicates time and effort to punching out letters on a keyboard to form a sentence or a paragraph will readily tell you that once the work is done the real challenge begins: how to put the result out into the world. As in every other creative sphere in the past half century, publishing has become commercialized to the point where the average, workaday wordsmith has minimal opportunities for publication in hard copy, whether in newspapers and journals or, still less likely, in the form of an actual published book. If the agency of publication sees no profit on the bottom line, you might as well forget it. Much really good writing never reaches a reading public, just as much good art never makes it to a gallery wall. That's the reality.

I have a friend and frequent critic who scoffs at the notion that a post on social media is equivalent to a publication. He sees it as a self-indulgence, at best a kind of self-help therapy, a search for validation from an already applauding audience. In the old way of thinking about publication, of course, he's right. There is no editorial process, no peer assessment, and little exposure to thoughtful criticism. But, again as a writer, I appreciate knowing that I can reach an admittedly small number of people who read what I write and derive some pleasure and value from it, and sometimes even take the trouble to respond. I like the back-and-forth, the post and comment, the possibility for a kind of conversation.

The cliché about conversation is that it's a lost art. It is certainly a rare and valued commodity these days, the gentle art of listening (or reading) and making a civil, thoughtful response at a time when all too frequently we shout so loudly at each other that we fail to hear what the other has to say. We talk about being "deep in conversation." What a lovely concept! And the more we converse, the deeper we get. So I say let's keep digging. Even on flighty social media, we can amaze, amuse, and challenge further thought. What does it matter if it's often purely personal? So what if I'm mostly preaching to the choir and hearing them sing back my song to me? Perhaps it's age, but I no longer believe in the seriousness and sanctity of the written word, as though every writer had something of importance to say. The words of a conversation are soon lost to the passing winds, and a good thing too.

I have committed recently to clearing out my storage boxes and trashing decades' worth of manuscripts, some of which have seen publication, many others not. How absurd to have preserved them all these years, as though some future scholar would come along to study the differences between first drafts, and second, and the published article. What silly arrogance! It will be a relief to see them go. And in the meantime,

I will keep publishing—no, more correctly, posting my passing thoughts on social media and put them out into the world where they will soon, inevitably, fade to silence in the same way as the sound of my voice. I will also be gratified to hear back from a few people who have bothered to read my words and have been moved by them, or sometimes angered, or challenged, or found in them some resonance that provokes response. I welcome any opportunity to embark on a conversation, even if happens only in the virtual space of online media. As I have said often enough before and will no doubt say again, it's the connection that counts.

This Is Not Me...

How to experience illness and pain without surrendering to them, without becoming their victim, without allowing them to become the center of my life? This has been my challenge in the past few weeks. It continues to challenge me, even though the illness that took over my body for a full month has now thankfully receded. I am no longer experiencing the debilitating symptoms of the upper respiratory infection that laid me low. The last of these was a lingering bad taste in the mouth and a persistent dizziness.

The pain is another matter. Last night, before bed, I was barely able to walk, attacked by a severe pain in the lower back that arrived from nowhere. Then there's the pain in my two new artificial hips and a new pain in the knee that has me worrying, now, about knee replacement. No getting around it, the body simply deteriorates as it ages. Everybody does it differently, for sure, but everybody does it. It's important, yes, to keep up with those things that benefit it, the exercise, the physical therapy, the proper foods, the right attitude. But pain is a stubborn rascal. It persists.

The important lesson, for me, and one that I keep having to learn afresh, is to avoid the suffering that accompanies pain when I'm unable to let it go. It's the suffering that threatens to rob me of my dignity. It leads me to complain, and it's a complaint—along with the self-pity that prompts it—that makes me a burden to myself and others. While pain is inevitable, the Buddhist dharma teaches, that suffering is optional. It results from attachment to the pain, identifying with it, dignifying it with my attention, and allowing it to define who I am.

I have learned that the great antidote to attachment is not denial, but release. It is not easy to practice, because pain is a powerful opponent and a persuasive one; it persuades me to forget what I know to be true. This is where meditation comes in because the attention required in meditation does not allow me to forget. In meditation, it is possible to put pain in its place. I repeat that great mantra of release: *this is not me, this is not mine, this is not who I am*. And I let go. The pain does not disappear; would that were so. Instead, it becomes something I am able to observe, dispassionately, without attachment, and its power over me diminishes. No longer resistant, vainly dismissive, hostile, and at war with myself, I can hope to make of pain my teacher and my friend.

A Nice Story

So here's a nice story for a change. Don't we all need one? The news about the nation and the world at large is mostly discouraging, but despite it all, there are good people. There is mutual respect and compassion. There is a sense of selfless service, a consideration of others.

Here is what happened one morning recently. It started some time ago when we began to notice that our trash cans, all three of them, black for trash, blue for recyclables and green for garden waste, were being mysteriously returned after pick-up each week to their place beside the fence to our neighbor's yard, where the remain hidden tidily out of sight from the street. Every Wednesday evening our gardener comes to wheel them out and leave them at the curb to await Thursday morning arrival the huge waste management trucks that lumber by; and, like dutiful neighbors, we have always replaced them where they belong when they are empty.

Until we no longer had to. When I went out to complete the weekly chore, I started to find them already back in their proper place. Closer observation confirmed that this little miracle would occur immediately after one of the trash trucks went by, so we concluded that it had been one of the drivers doing us this favor. Watching the trash cans up and down the street, we could tell that he was doing it only for us, not our neighbors, and of course, we couldn't help but wonder why.

Come Christmas time Ellie and I agreed that our benefactor should get a gift to thank him for these weekly acts of kindness. We rarely see him because he arrives early and is quickly gone, so it seemed best to enclose a modest gift with a card and a message to convey our gratitude and to get up earlier than usual in hopes of catching him in the act. The night before I pinned the envelope to the fence where I thought that he'd be sure to find it if we missed him.

    I woke up early on trash pickup morning and could not go back to sleep. Instead, I lay waiting for the inimitable rumble of the trash truck and the deafening crash of trash cans being hoisted, their content emptied into its bowels. So I was ready to run upstairs (our bedroom is on the lower floor in our hillside house) as soon as I heard the first truck arrive. It was the wrong one. The driver picked up one of our three cans and revved up again to continue on his way. The second one, as it turned out, was also the wrong one, picking up the trash on the other side of the street and headed the other way. But I struck it lucky with the arrival of the third! I sneaked a peek out of our front door and there he was, a huge Black man—a true gentle giant, it turned out—who climbed down from his cab and started to wheel our trash cans back out of sight.

    I caught up with him just as he found my envelope pinned to the fence. He must have sensed my approach because he turned with a big friendly grin and stuck out a massive paw to shake my hand. The man dwarfed me. He was tall, yes, and built like a refrigerator. And every cubic inch of him oozed kindness. He just radiated the stuff, like Santa Claus, but without the white beard and the ho-ho-ho. "How's the wife?" he asked me cheerfully, explaining that he often sees her on her walks around the neighborhood and they always exchange a friendly wave.

    Our friend was grateful for the gift—as grateful as we are to him, not only for his weekly act of kindness but also for restoring our sense that human beings can actually care about other human beings and go out of their way to help. I asked him the obvious question, the one we had often pondered in recent weeks and months: Why? Why us? Why no one else along the street? What made us so privileged to receive this kindness?

"Well," he told me. "I seen you." Ellie and I are of a respectable age! "I seen your wife, too, dragging those big trash bins back, and I couldn't let that happen."

I thanked him again, from a full heart, and he swallowed up my hand again in his before climbing back into his cab and heading off to the next house down the street. Sentimental codger that I am, I found myself shedding a tear or two as I headed back downstairs to share the story with Ellie. After which, we no longer had the heart to turn on the television as we usually do, to watch the morning news.

WWBD?

I find myself asking this question more and more frequently these days. What would Buddha do to maintain his gentle smile and imperturbable peace of mind when surrounded by so much chaos, so much divisiveness, so much in the political and social environment that is venal and abusive? So much animosity and oppression? Such skewed values, so much violence, so much incitement of others to violence? And a world in turmoil everywhere?

I call myself "an aspiring Buddhist" because I am not a religious man. Still, rather late in life, I was led to deeply respect the Buddha, whose teachings are a fine model for a life of truth, compassion, and the kind of happiness that harms no one and does not come at the cost of our fellow human or other living beings. I balk only when it comes to notions of rebirth and multiple series of lives to be lived before enlightenment.

That said, I was also brought up with a social and political conscience that will not allow me to stand by when I see injustice, inequity, and exploitation, let alone tyranny. I came to America as an immigrant more than a half-century ago, attracted by what I thought to be a more democratic society than my native land, where I was pigeon-holed by my public-school Oxbridge accent as soon as I opened my mouth to speak, both by those born far above me on the inescapable, centuries-old social ladder and those born on a lower rung. I was delighted, for example, that the attendant who pumped my gas when I first came to America (there were such men of service in those days!) seemed to think no less of himself than a Rockefeller for the nature of his work or the accent of his speech.

Was this a romantic notion? Perhaps. But to this newly immigrant European every American seemed confident that where they stood was no more than a stepping stone to still greater opportunities and a better life, for both themselves and their families.

How things have changed! The tiresome class consciousness that was in part responsible for my decision to leave my home country has taken root over here in a yet more virulent, angry, and antagonistic form. The divisions are more convoluted: they exist not only between upper and lower or between professional and working classes but between political affiliations, racial identities, wealth and poverty, coast and midland, city and rural, in an ever-changing shuffle of conflicting loyalties.

All this exists in the context of noxious national political melodrama and a never-ending series of international crises, enough to challenge the mind that seeks nothing other than peace and justice for all, and the equanimity that comes with knowing that each of us is striving for the same. So the aspiring Buddhist asks himself this question: what would the Buddha do? And for the writer like me who feels a nagging obligation to use his work to make a difference: what would the Buddha say?

As to the latter, I have the guidance of the Buddha's "Eightfold Path" that leads to the end of suffering. It's called Right Speech, one of the five precepts of ethical conduct. The Buddha defined it as "abstinence from false speech, abstinence from malicious speech, abstinence from harsh speech, and abstinence from idle chatter." His definition might be interpreted thus: Don't lie, don't be nasty, don't be rude, and perhaps, in this day and age, don't use Twitter. Or don't gossip. None of which forbids me from telling the truth as I see it. It does not prohibit calling a man a liar if he keeps telling lies. It is not malicious to call someone out for unethical behavior. The Buddha himself is known to have resorted to harsh speech when it came to addressing ignorance or cruelty. Right Speech, as I understand it, does not require me to be mealy-mouthed.

Speaking out forthrightly, speaking the truth without malice or harsh words, and with unflinching honesty when addressing mean-spirited or misguided actions is a social and ethical obligation, whether personal or political. It is also a reliable means to calm the troubled mind and rid myself of otherwise toxic thoughts and feelings. I believe the Buddha would approve of this kind of truth-telling when it condemns wrongful words or actions. He did not require anyone to be silent in the face of mischief.

Other than Right Speech, what would the Buddha have me do?

Not lie down and take it. Not submit to tyranny. Not allow myself to be the proverbial doormat. He would urge me, surely, to intervene when I am witness to injustice, abuse, and exploitation. I am not permitted by the teachings of the Buddha to walk by on the other side like the Levite in the gospel story of the Good Samaritan. And it is painful to observe, in today's Trumpworld, how many self-professed Christians are willing to disavow the obligation Jesus taught and instead embrace the "prosperity Gospel" of self-enrichment—which Jesus would surely have condemned.

If I hear rightly what the Buddha taught, he would have me practice goodwill and compassion toward all my fellow beings, not only those with whom I agree but also those with whom I radically disagree. This would include the Trumpeters whose loyalty to their cult leader sanctions racial bias, social division, and a callous disregard for the less fortunate: the poor, the sick, the homeless—and the immigrant. The practice of *metta*, requiring me to send out thoughts of goodwill even to those I dislike is challenging at a time when we see callousness and even cruelty abound.

Yet this, as I understand it, is precisely what the Buddha would have us do. To follow his express injunction and send out such thoughts even to the person we may secretly despise is not to approve hurtful words or harmful actions and, counterintuitively perhaps, I find it healing to rid mind and body of the animosity that is harmful mostly to myself. In sacrificing my anger, no matter how righteous, I release the toxins that poison my bloodstream. As a bonus, if my good wishes do happen to reach my nemesis in some unknowable way and somehow touch his or her heart, even possibly sparking a second, less disagreeable thought, I will have done myself no disfavor. Quite the opposite. And if not, there is nothing lost—unless perhaps a burdensome chunk of ego.

Such is the wisdom of the Buddha. It is wisdom I aspire to, but often fail to put into practice. I repeat the familiar words, *May those I dislike find true happiness in their lives.* Which does not presume to tell them what to think or how to live their lives, but more so, to remind me of where my own happiness lies.

November 2015

I remember waking up in shock and horror that morning in November 2000, the day that George W. Bush was virtually appointed to the presidency by a 5-4 vote of the US Supreme Court. How was such a thing possible? Worse, I thought four years later, was his re-election in 2004, even after his disastrous invasion of Iraq and his refusal to pay for his war with taxes on the wealthy. His munificence on behalf of those who did not need it was offensive. Had we Americans learned nothing about the man in his first four years in office, I reasoned? Or did reason and commonsense no longer count?

This inner turmoil awoke my need to take charge and fix things: what can I do, I asked myself, other than wring my hands in despair? *What can I do?*

A wordsmith by trade, I began casting about for the words that would show me the way and it was this old habit that led me, by sheer serendipity, into the blogosphere. This was 2004, remember, when blogs were not yet widely known. I was easily seduced. Even I, I discovered to my delight, even I could create a blog, despite my unfamiliarity with the digital world. Following a handful of easy online instructions, I first had to decide on a title. My fingers seemed to act of their own volition on the keyboard as I typed in the words: "The Bush Diaries." Mere moments later I found myself working on the first of what were to be many subsequent, almost daily, letters to the President—letters that were not unkind but irreverent, a teasing rebuke for the error of his ways.

Once engaged, I kept at it for the next four years of the Bush presidency. Well, almost four years. The letters were never sent, of course, but posted online for a growing readership, and later published as a book. But there came a time, after several years and literally hundreds of these letters, when I woke up one day with the realization that I had begun to find Bush in bed with me every day! On that same day, "The Bush Diaries" expired, and the blog morphed effortlessly into "The Buddha Diaries", a much more congenial effort that occupied my attention for close to 10 years!

Now, all those years later, I woke in November 2015 with the same feeling of dread as when Bush was elected. I was shocked, horrified by the election results. We Americans had ignored every warning sign and had voted—incredibly, to my mind—in favor of the anger, ignorance, and intolerance that the President-elect had appealed to during his campaign; we had collectively voted for a man who was (and still is, to my mind) plainly narcissistic, willfully ignorant, authoritarian, and willing to exploit such evils as misogyny and racism in his greed for power. How could that be?

That old "what can I do?" impulse overwhelmed me once again, that old sense of despair and the anger at those who failed to see things the way I do—the *right* way! But even though "The Bush Diaries" had for a while satisfied that need to "do something," I swore there would be no Trump Diaries. This time, I was sensible enough to recognize that I can't just arrange the world the way I want it; everything that happens in the world out there is beyond my control. Sometimes things will go my way and sometimes not, and I am not given to decide which outcome is which. The only thing over which I exercise a modicum of control is what happens in my mind.

Like it or not, there was a new reality we had to deal with. If I chose to ignore it, I risked inhabiting the kind of bubble I attributed to those with whom I disagreed. There is so much anger, so much fear, so much chaos, not only in our country, but in the world at large. I cannot change this reality or control it. What I *can* do, acknowledging the chaos out there to be no more than a reflection of the chaos within, is recognize that my best contribution to healing the sickness in the world is to work on clearing the morass of anxiety, anger, grief and fear that obscures the clarity of my own mind and distorts my vision. If I allow myself to attach to my fears and judgments and cling to them, I will accomplish nothing but to project them out into the world and succeed only in making these complex matters worse.

In the new circumstance of that morning, I remembered Voltaire's well-meaning but clueless naïf, Candide. With the last of his illusions shattered, he finally comes to understand that his only option is to "*cultiver son jardin*"—to cultivate his garden. The garden I need to cultivate is my mind. It's up to me to tend it carefully, no matter what happens in the world beyond my reach. "Always look on the bright side of life," sang the chorus at the end of Monty Python's "Life of Brian", with dozens of Jesus figures agonizing on their crucifixes. The one benefit I could take from the election of the abominable Donald Trump as the "leader of the free world" was the decision to clear my mind of the weeds that had been growing there untamed, thanks to my indulgence and neglect; or, to mix metaphors, to polish my mirror of the world out there in order to reflect it with greater truthfulness and equanimity. To do otherwise, I concluded, was to contribute to the chaos that I saw.

The Internet

The partnership of science and technology has created a new nuclear weapon of mass destruction called the Internet. A force that had the potential to promote so much good in the world has been co-opted by the insatiable greed of our benighted species to ends that threaten to destroy us.

I have been reading newspaper reports—I get my news in the old-fashioned way, but nowadays online!—about the multiple ways in which social media were misused in recent elections and threaten to loom even larger in the coming one. "Fake news" stories, rapidly promulgated and gobbled up by the gullible, succeed in misleading millions of voters with false information before being discredited, and then only after inestimable damage is done. Abetted by the Russian government in 2015, Wikileaks selectively released one candidate's private emails to the public with the express intent of causing her embarrassment, obstructing her campaign, and promoting that of her opponent. It's reasonable to wonder what that rival's email history might have looked like, had it received similar treatment. Instead, and just as harmfully, Twitter provided Trump with instantaneous access to millions of followers for his toxic screed and other social media offered a convenient loudspeaker and platform for anyone with hateful views to share or arguments to make, while honest, thoughtful posts could rapidly be exposed to instant vilification by coordinated armies of opponents.

The possible election of a manifestly uninformed, unqualified candidate to the most influential office in the world is testament to the damage already done, based in good part on the almost instantaneous, venomous spread of lies that, absent the immediacy of the Internet, would otherwise be subject to reasonable critical appraisal and timely rebuttal. Only in today's world could such things happen.

Like it or not, the infinite power of the Internet has been unleashed upon our planet, at a time when the planet itself is vulnerable. As with nuclear weapons, humankind, our toddler species, has found a treacherous new toy to play with. Without vigilance and a sober, adult sense of responsibility, we are liable to destroy this vulnerable nursery of ours with our childish games.

The Hand

I'm interested in revisiting an old debate, the one that has to do with the human hand in artmaking. Here's what prompted me: I recently spent the afternoon with my grandson at the Kidspace Children's Museum in Pasadena, near the Rose Bowl, and on emerging from the museum toward the end of the afternoon, I noticed a number of young people wandering about with laptops, scanning the landscape, or sitting in small groups bent over their devices, intent on whatever it was they were doing.

My first thought was that this was a science project of some kind, perhaps to track the flight patterns of birds or determine the geological substructure of the soil. But no. Once my curiosity finally overcame my reticence, I asked one of these young people what was so engaging them.

They were painting. This was a class from the nearby Art Center College of Design, whose assignment was to go out and make plein-air landscape paintings. On laptops. Using drop-down menus for color palettes and brushstroke choices and scribbling away with genius pens on the surface of their electronic tablets. I took a careful look at a couple of the results as they appeared on their monitors and, yes, they looked a whole lot like the plein air paintings of the early California Impressionists. When printed up on heavy paper or canvas they could be made to look like a watercolor, a pastel or an oil painting, take your pick. Minus, of course, the surface texture of the medium. But as one of the students confidently informed me, "They're working on that."

It's in part the texture of a painting that I love. It's the evidence of the human hand, the passion, the virtuosity, the tactile immediacy. It's the heartbeat of a fellow human being who has experienced something akin to what I myself experience on Planet Earth; who has seen the things that I have seen, with a passion that compels a person to record them in a unique and individual way. Nothing else like this particular painting has ever existed before or will ever be made again.

I am not ill-informed. I have been observing the art world and its changes for several decades now and am well aware that art is more than ever mass-produced, manufactured, computer-generated, or created in many other intriguing ways that do not involve the human hand. Photography, film, and video have become important and legitimate ways for artists to realize their vision. Critics, teachers, and aesthetic theorists alike have managed to provide the new media with impressive rationales; some even mock traditional art forms as redundant or passé.

Okay, I get it. But when the hand is removed from the equation, that vital connection with the heart can easily be lost. I may be going a bit soft in the head with my advancing years, but I find that I'm inclined to listen less to the intellect than the heart when I'm looking to art for the best it has to offer. My head is fed in so many ways in the contemporary world, be it in word, image or sound, it positively aches with the surfeit of information I receive. When confronted with a computer image, it's essentially data that I'm asked to process—a function of the brain. What happens to the heart?

The same might be argued for the hand-painted image on the museum or gallery wall: as visual information, it too must be received and processed by the brain. But pixels are not paint. They have no substance. As the artist David Hockey once remarked they are simply *thin*. My first contact with contemporary art resulted from a fascination with conceptual and post-conceptual work. Now I'm beginning to think that once you "get the idea" there's nothing more to get. I find myself wanting more. I like *thick* stuff, art that is thickly textured with meanings and associations, with images and references. Otherwise, I find it rather thin gruel. It's made to be consumed. And no matter that it's tasty, like a piece of candy or a potato chip, it all comes out the other end as the same old shit.

Call me sentimental, but I still want to be *moved* by a work of art—and by "moved" I mean not just emotionally, but to a different place, a new understanding of the world. I want it to speak to my whole humanity, not just to the part that's located in between my ears. I want to feel it in the flesh, a physical sensation. I want to feel it in the heart and, if you'll forgive the expression, the soul. Integrity is a concept that's important to me, and for me integrity—in art as it is in life—is wholeness. A person of integrity is he or she in whom intellect, body, emotion, and—for want of a better word—spirit, are aligned in a harmonious balance and who act, and react, accordingly.

Coincidentally, on the same day as my encounter with those students—and this is not to criticize or minimize their work, but rather an attempt to examine the thoughts and feelings it aroused—I happened to visit the home of some very old friends who are ardent collectors of what these days we call tribal art. (I'm happy that the insulting term "primitive" was retired a long time ago.) The powerful blend of form and social function in those wooden carvings, the (hand!) craft involved in their making, the ritual that once characterized their use, the imposing quality of their physical presence—all these add up to something that does, yes, engage the intellect but is also profoundly moving in the sense I have attempted to describe.

Art, for me, is first and foremost a way of learning more about what it means to be a human being. I learn not only more about the "hand" that made it but, through what it has to say about its maker's very different life experience, more about my own. To that end there is nothing so sensitive as the human hand, nor indeed so complex in its operations, so dexterous, so able to able to establish or express meaning through the simple medium of touch. Hand to heart, heart to brain, and back again to heart. It's not my intention to dismiss the value of other media, but I still find this to be the most gratifying reward in my relationship with art.

My Commencement Speech

Not that any self-respecting university would think of inviting me, a reformed academic now nearly thirty years in recovery, but I do have thoughts around this annual graduation time about what I'd want to say to the generation just now stepping out into the adult world. (I left the academic world—or, more truthfully, was given the boot—back in 1986. I have never been tempted to return and am thankful now that I saw the light. No disrespect to academia, but it was not the place for me.) Still, if some institution were so ill-advised as to invite me, here in a few words is what I would want to say to the graduating class:

Don't neglect your inner life.

I'd like to think that some part of a university education requires you to pay attention to the responsibility of simply being a human being, whether in a Shakespeare seminar or a social studies class, a course in environmental sciences or comparative religion. In recent years, however, the value of a degree in the humanities has been called into question, and for the obvious practical reasons: after investing so much time and money in a college degree, what in the name of Sophocles will you be able to do in life with a bachelor's degree in, say, English literature?

In part because of the expense of that undergraduate degree, we have come to consider a university education little more than a training ground for a future career. The first order of business when you emerge from the hallowed halls with that piece of paper in your hand is to find a job that pays the kind of money you need to pay off the debt you undoubtedly accumulated along the way. This is a daunting challenge, as we know, in today's job market. Kudos to those who manage it. But the sober truth is that most young people emerging from college will be lucky simply to get by financially without help, at least for the first few years.

Even then, there are other things to worry about; finding a place to live that fits a meager budget; finding a partner, if that's what you're looking for; starting a family, though most prefer to wait for much longer than was the case for my generation; and then soon having to provide for their welfare and education. All the while working to climb the ladder towards whatever you think of as success. None of it is easy, all of it demanding on your time and energy.

It is easy, in all this, to neglect the inner life. And yet, as I look back on the progress of my own life from the perspective of, yes, an octogenarian, I regret having neglected this aspect of my life for far too long. And the truth is, I might have gone on blithely neglecting it forever, but that I was brought up short, as are so many in middle age, by an attack of painful existential turmoil that forced me to pause a while and take a good look at what was happening within. By which I mean in my heart, mind and soul.

I had a lot of catch-up work to do. Thirty years later I still have work to do. I can look back and tell myself that I should have started earlier. I didn't. I was too busy doing those other things, the ones I mentioned just a moment ago. It is also true to say that by this time, after years of neglect, I was intimidated by the thought of what I'd find if I looked too deep inside. I had stored up decades of old fears and resentments, anger, and grief, feelings of confusion, insecurity and doubt. I had never understood that there was a cost to tamping these things down and keeping them where I could hide them or deny them, and where others could not see; I did not understand that these feelings do not simply go away. Unseen, unexpressed, they hang around and often end up causing endless pain not only for yourself but also, destructively, for those around you—even those you love. You don't understand how much hard work is involved in keeping them all repressed down there in the darkness, and that work manifests in your life as stress. You may find yourself self-medicating, commonly with alcohol or drugs, but also with work, or sex, or other forms of addiction. The longer you keep them inside, the more likely they are to cause physical as well as emotional pain.

So the work is to keep looking fearlessly inside, to know what's going on in there. It took me until halfway through my life—though who knows what half a life is?—before I came to understand that it was governed by buried memories and the powerful unconscious emotions associated with them. I was fortunate to be confronted with the damage they had caused, no matter how uncomfortable, because that was when the work began: for the first time in my life, I began to take the inner life seriously.

What does the work look like? Well, it is unflinching honesty, a hard look at the things you hide, repress, deny. For some it will take the form of therapy. For others, like myself, the help of tough peers who are further along the path. Others still, finally recognizing they can't do it alone, end up in organizations like Alcoholics Anonymous. Some are even able to do the work alone, in the isolation of retreats. We all have a dark side, no exceptions. We all need to look at it and see it for what it is. And then we need to disempower it by exposing it to the light. Best to start early, though. The dark gets darker, more impenetrable as you age.

So there you have it, in a nutshell. Whatever else you do in life, *don't neglect your inner life.* Or, as Sophocles put it with admirable simplicity centuries ago; Know thyself. The reward is as simple as it is invaluable: the happiness that comes with freedom. Freedom from fear and anger. Freedom from the demons that dwell within. The freedom to live the best life that awaits you if you dare.

A Fall

Ellie and I were confronted with a nasty reminder that we octogenarians need to exercise due caution when out walking, especially after dark. Ellie was out with Jake the dog just after sunset last night when she tripped and took a fall a couple of blocks from our house. Luckily, she had her phone with her and called me, in obvious distress and pain...

Luckily too, even while she was on the phone to me, a passing Good Samaritan spotted her struggling to get up and stopped his truck to help. Much confusion followed. With the phone line still open I could half-overhear what was going on and kept trying to ask if my help was needed. I finally managed to speak to the man who was helping her, and who happened to have been a close neighbor across the street from us a few years ago. He assured me he would drive Ellie home.

After many expressions of gratitude and much stumbling around in the dark, I had her home again and we sat debating the need for medical attention. She had fallen face down and had a small but still bleeding wound at the corner of her left eye, along with what would clearly turn out to be a significant shiner. The prospect of a trip to an emergency room and hours of sitting around in a busy hospital waiting room was uninviting, and the only two urgent care clinics in Laguna Beach were already closed. What to do?

We first called a few neighbors to see if they had medical or nursing contacts who could help, at least with an initial evaluation and informed advice. Finding none, we settled on a trek to a more remote urgent care clinic that we discovered online, a few miles south, dropped Jake off with friends, and set off into the night.

Everyone at the clinic was wonderful. The only initial aggravation was the one to be expected: reams of paperwork covering medical history, insurance, permissions, and God knows what else. Pages and pages of it. The receptionist supervised, sympathetically. Once past that hurdle, the nurse was kind, concerned, attentive. When he finally made his appearance, the doctor, too, was friendly, full of the kind of jokes he must have made a thousand times before. He gave Ellie a couple of painful numbing injections around the eye before patching up the wound and sealing it with a couple of stitches. We had made a good choice, he told us—we already knew—to seek medical help and get attention to the wound. While there were no symptoms of concussion, it was always best to be sure.

So there we were. We drove home, picked up the dog, made ourselves a bowl of soup, watched a harmless show about smart pets on the television, and went to bed in good time. When I checked up on Ellie early the next morning—I always wake up long before she does—she managed a weary reassurance before falling back asleep. I noted an already very black eye, but I am deeply grateful that her fall resulted in nothing more serious than this. When she tripped and took that fall on an uneven sidewalk a couple of years ago, remember the result was a broken hip, surgery, and a long period of recuperation. So this was a helpful and necessary reminder that we octogenarians must be circumspect when we venture out after dark.

Lying

I have a new baseball cap. The words on the front, above the brim, read: MAKE LYING WRONG AGAIN—a play, obviously, on the MAKE AMERICA GREAT AGAIN slogan. My cap is, purposely, not red, but gray. I wouldn't want to create the wrong impression. But this does put me in mind of another story.

I am an immigrant. It's worth saying again because of what I left behind me, and what I came to find. It's also worth saying to remind myself of the predicament in which so many thousands of human beings find themselves today, waiting at the border for admission to the country they believe with all their hearts could offer them a better life. America is famously the land of immigrants, but a vocal minority of Americans today—many of them immigrants or the sons and daughters of immigrants, or at least their grandchildren—are fiercely resistant to allowing others in.

I first left England, my native country, in 1959, and spent 2 years in Germany and two years in Canada before moving to Iowa in 1964. I was attracted to this country because it offered me the kind of opportunity I could not find elsewhere. In my case, the opportunity was to become the writer I had always wanted to be. Writers, I discovered to my surprise, were welcomed in the academic world, in particular at the University of Iowa, where I joined the renowned Writers Workshop. People joined together to make it possible for me to come there, a young writer with a growing family and no visible means of support. I was offered a grant, a teaching position, inexpensive housing, all because I wrote... poetry! I could not believe my good fortune.

When I arrived, I found myself surrounded by writers from all parts of the world; Japan, Cambodia, India, Turkey, as well as a veritable alphabet of European countries. We were all welcomed, valued for the special qualities we brought, the languages we spoke and used in our work as writers, the literary heritages from which we worked. There was equal respect for all traditions, every culture, every background. This was the America I had dreamed of! Looking back on it, my introduction to this country was remarkable. And while I am sure there are still pockets where this cosmopolitan embrace still thrives, I am sad to see so much xenophobia, so much angry rejection of difference in America today.

My own background continued to serve me well in my professional life. My British education was respected, valued. My accent alone was the source of entirely undeserved professional advancement: if I was so articulate, so well-spoken, I had to be unusually smart and competent! And the impression I managed to convey was in some respects true: the experience I brought from childhood, school, and university years in England allowed me to add my own drop to the great American cultural bucket. When I wrote about art and artists, for example, as I did for many years, it was always with that peculiar English accent and a way of looking at things that was shaped by centuries of European history and literary traditions foreign to my American peers.

I became a citizen in 1972, nearly ten years after my arrival. I felt foolish living here and not being able to vote. It was time to take on a more fully responsible role in the country in which I was obviously by now a permanent resident. I was shocked, in the process of naturalization, and honestly more than a little amused to learn that lying was a virtual prerequisite if I wished to qualify as an American. Let me explain. I had no difficulty at first in honestly affirming that I was not now nor ever had been... that old question about Communism, which seemed to me absurd, but there you are. But then there were questions on the form that had to be answered under penalty of perjury: Had I ever knowingly committed a crime, for instance? Well, yes. I had smoked a good deal of marijuana; I may even have sold some to friends for their enjoyment when I had some and they didn't. I certainly knew that to be illegal at the time. However, it would obviously foul up the works if I admitted to this crime, so I answered No. There were questions, too, about very personal morality to which a truthful answer might have exposed me to rejection. What business was this of the US government anyway? So I lied, choosing to avoid complicating my application by committing another crime. This time it was perjury.

It seemed to me then and still seems today to be a rather delicious irony: to qualify as a good American I had to lie—the title of an op-ed piece I wrote for the Los Angeles Times and for which they agreed to break their own rule and publish anonymously. To date, the authorities have not caught up with me for my crime and I remain at liberty, a free American. But only thanks to my lie.

The Mute-E

Speaking of the University of Iowa, where I spent my final year as Instructor of the International Translation Workshop, working with poets from throughout the world, here's something you probably never needed to know...

The French language has a magical gift whose equivalent we completely lack in English: it's the mute-e at the end of a French word that is both pronounced and not pronounced, creating a kind of subtle presence in its absence, a soundless sound, if you can imagine.

One of my favorite examples is the last line of *L'Étranger*, a prose poem by Charles Baudelaire. An importunate questioner has been pestering the stranger with questions about what he loves and receiving only enigmatic evasions by way of answers. At last, exasperated—or simply resigned, depending on your point of view—the questioner asks, in translation, "So what it is that you do love, extraordinary stranger?" And the stranger answers, in the French original, "*J'aime les nuages, les nuages qui passent, là-bas, là-bas. J'aime les nuages...*"

In its inadequate, pedestrian English translation, that line would read: "I love the clouds, the passing clouds, over yonder, over yonder." But the English totally fails to capture the magic of those mute-e's at the end of the words—*J'aime, nuages, nuages, passent, aime, nuages*—sounds which are, precisely, there and not there, pronounced and not pronounced, a magical presence which lifts them out of the mundane into, well... the clouds. They are mysterious, atmospheric, numinous. They leave you, with the poem, wondering…

A bit esoteric, perhaps. Apologies. I have no idea why these thoughts came to me this morning.

After the Shooting in Las Vegas: A Buddhist Litany

I mourn the loss of 59 innocent lives and the wounding of over 500 more.

I send thoughts of goodwill and compassion to the families and loved ones of all those who died;

I send thoughts of goodwill and compassion to the loved ones of the perpetrator, who also died. May they be free from pain and suffering, may they find equanimity;

I send thoughts of goodwill and compassion to the loved ones of all those wounded by the gunman's bullets;

I send thoughts of goodwill and compassion to all those who came to their aid, the police and the paramedics and other law enforcement and medical officials;

I send thoughts of goodwill and compassion to those who worked tirelessly in the hospitals to save lives;

I send thoughts of goodwill and compassion to all those who suffer from the abuse of deadly weapons. May they know the power of peace and forgiveness;

I send thoughts of goodwill and compassion to those who own firearms and campaign for the protection of their rights. May their intentions be free from ill will and animosity;

I send thoughts of goodwill and compassion to those who militate for the reasonable regulation of firearms, their possession and use;

I send thoughts of goodwill and compassion to those who manufacture and market the weapons used to kill and injure innocents;

I send thoughts of goodwill and compassion to those empowered to legislate the possession and use of such weapons.

May we all abjure the use of violence in our lives; may we all find the path to peace, mutual tolerance, goodwill, and happiness.

The Gift of Art

I can't help but wonder what my late father-in-law would have thought about the controversy surrounding the new campus for the Los Angeles County Museum of Art, now under construction at its Wilshire Boulevard location. This is not an idle question because Mike loved the museum and was himself among its substantial benefactors. A novelist and a screenwriter of modest wealth, he could never have matched the generosity of major benefactors, but he gave significantly in his way.

Michael Blankfort spent the better part of his life in Los Angeles. Aside from his avocation as a writer, his passion was contemporary art. Together with his wife Dorothy, he put together a collection that was considered an important one, though without being huge or splashy. His discerning eye and sense for the integrity and aesthetic value of an artist's work drew him to purchase things he loved—paintings, particularly—long before their value soared into the stratosphere. With the encouragement of pioneer professionals like Walter (Chico) Hopps and Henry Hopkins and along with a core group of budding collectors in the late 1950s and early 1960s, Mike and Dossy, as she was universally known, were regular patrons at cutting-edge galleries like Virginia Dwan and Ferus, purchasing work by artists like Jasper Johns, Yves Klein, Richard Diebenkorn, Willem de Kooning and Franz Kline long before the art market would put their work beyond their reach.

I think it's fair to say that Michael and Dorothy were courted by LACMA. They were enthusiastic supporters of the institution from the start and leaders in early support groups for contemporary art and artists. Michael was eventually appointed to the museum's board and was proud to be involved in its decision-making process. In time, the couple agreed to bequeath the major part of their collection to the museum and their decision was rewarded with a special exhibition, "The Michael and Dorothy Blankfort Collection" in 1982, along with the publication of a handsome catalog in celebration of their gift. Mike wrote a wonderful, engagingly personal introduction which he titled, wittily, *Confessions of an Art Eater (With Apologies to Thomas de Quincey)*. Their gift, while financially modest at the time, would be valued in today's market in the multi-millions of dollars.

I do not presume, of course, to speak for the Blankforts about LACMA so long after they left us, but I can't resist the speculation. Mike, I know, was an institutionalist at heart, and would incline intellectually toward support for the museum's establishment—its board and its director. But he was, too, perhaps paradoxically, an old-time, 1930s East Coast socialist, and his gift was motivated in good part by a sense of civic obligation. The paintings, he would remind us, were only provisionally in his possession: they belonged to everyone. So his thinking would surely have been swayed by the later director Michael Govan's vision of satellite locations, where the museum's collection would be accessible to disparate, localized audiences.

In this context, it was clearly the Blankforts' intention for the works in their collection to be available to the public. Given that it includes often small, if choice examples of a well-known artist's work, however, many items from the collection are already exhibited less frequently than the donors would have hoped, and the planned overall reduction in exhibition space at the proposed new LACMA (a loss of some 10,000 square feet, if my understanding is correct) will likely further reduce any possibility that they will be regularly seen. The prospect of those precious art objects languishing in the basement or in some remote warehouse is painful to both of Mike's surviving daughters. They were bequeathed in order to enrich the museum's collection of the best of human creativity on permanent display, and the architectural plan now in process offers less access to that broad sweep of the art historical record that is the mission of an encyclopedic museum like LACMA.

Finally—and this is frankly more speculative still—would Mike and Dossy shudder as many do at the mid-century, Googie architecture motel look of the proposed new LACMA? It's presumably intended but nowhere near a majestic sweep across the city's main thoroughfare? Its thumb in the eye of the kind of conventional exhibition space where their collection was honored in that 1982 event? We can't know, of course. But we think it quite possible that we speak in the name of other families of donors who have good cause to worry that gifts that bear the names of their parents or grandparents will be subject to disrespect or negligence because of changes now underway.

With all goodwill for our local museum, there are many who are disappointed by what appears to be its new direction. Count me among them.

Hide, Repress, Deny

I learned long ago that it is the things we hide, repress, and deny that cause us the greatest harm. At the intimate, personal level, they lie buried in our bodies and our minds, still active, festering, without our being aware of their harmful effects. It takes an effort to bring them back to consciousness if we want to heal them. Old childhood wounds are the prime example. We all carry them. The happiest among us and those best adjusted to adult life are those who have learned in some way to expose them to the light and the air they need to heal. Those who fail to do so often end up crippled by physical pain, emotional debility, or addiction.

These thoughts come to mind this morning as I reflect on the damage wrought by what the leader of our powerful political parties has sought to hide, repress, and deny in his personal life. We don't need to be armchair psychotherapists to guess that there is something amiss in the emotional makeup of a man who is so addicted to lies that his presidency was marked by more than 30,000 of them, by the count of observers who watch his words more closely than I do; who swings wildly between rage at others and self-aggrandizement; who, having acquired a position of the greatest responsibility, repudiates it outright when faced with the consequences of his actions.

The history of his time in office and his actions since show the far-reaching, national, international consequences of this man's propensity to hide, repress, deny. The tragic arc of the Covid crisis, for example, makes it clear that he was well informed of facts that were vital to the health and well-being of the people he was elected to serve, and that he hid them, knowingly repressing information that could have saved countless lives; that he willfully refused to listen to public health authorities, medical expertise, and the science that could have curtailed, if not halted the spread of the pandemic.

I am not a Christian, but I was brought up in the church. I recall that it was Jesus himself, whose words and deeds engendered the Christian faith, told his followers, "You will know the truth, and the truth will set you free." We live under the spell of a man to whom the truth is foreign, even dangerous, the very thing he has learned to hide, repress, and deny. We are witness to the catastrophic consequences of his words and actions.

The urgent question we now face is this: with such immeasurable damage done and trust so severely undermined among so many of our fellow citizens, what will it take to restore the respect for truth, plain facts, and science that we will need to address the challenges we face and find a good path forward? A candid acknowledgment and healing of past wounds are needed if we are to return to sanity—let alone compassion. This is challenging and arduous work. Is it work that we are willing to undertake?

Apropos…
… of nothing.

The burning question for me in the middle of the night last night was this: who performed the marriage ceremony for the Owl and the Pussycat?

Who knows why I woke with the Edward Lear jingle in mind? Why I had to silently recite the whole damn thing, to see if I could remember it? But that's how it was. I lay there going through it, line by line. I remembered almost all of it. The "beautiful pea green boat," the "honey and plenty of money/wrapped up in a five-pound note." I remembered the Owl's words as he sang to his small guitar: "Oh lovely Pussy, Oh Pussy my love, What a beautiful Pussy you are, you are." And the Pussycat's response: "Oh, let us be married, too long we have tarried. But what shall we do for a ring?" Then, yes…

> *They sailed away for a year and a day,*
> *to the land where the bong tree grows.*
> *And there in a wood,*
> *a piggy wig stood,*
> *with a ring at the end of his nose,*
> *his nose,*
> *his nose,*
> *With a ring at the end of his nose*

Ah! A solution to their problem!

> *Dear Pig, are you willing,*

> *to sell for one shilling, your ring?*
> *Said the Piggy, I will.*
> *So they took it away*
> *and were married next day*
> *By the…*

And this is where I ran into a brick wall. For the life of me, I could not remember who married them, except that he "lived on a hill." I tussled for a long time with my memory, but it would not yield up the secret. I did remember that "they dined on mince and slices of quince, and danced by the light of the moon." But who played that minister?

Memory failed me. I had to resort to Google this morning. Of course. It was "the turkey who lived on the hill."

The turkey!

It's the important things like this that keep my mind occupied these days My memory for such things never fails to amaze me. Perhaps it's the rhymes…

Good Looking

Meditation is an art. I was fortunate to have been led to the practice many years ago, and now take a great deal of pleasure in sharing the experience with others when I can. I have put together a friendly group of neighbors on our Franklin Hill at the east end of Hollywood and we have been meeting every Wednesday evening since 2016—on Zoom, through the time of Covid—to sit together for a guided meditation.

There is a nexus, I have also discovered, between the art of meditation and the other kind, the kind we enjoy in museums and galleries. Most of us like to look at paintings and to have art of one kind or another on our walls. I worked professionally for many years as an art critic for national magazines and flattered myself to be something of an expert... until I began to realize to my dismay, after years of meditation, that I was hardly looking at the paintings I had the chutzpah to write about.

This is an experience common to many an art lover: you find yourself surrounded by paintings in a white-walled gallery, say, and give a quick glance around before you start your tour, pausing here and there for a better look at one painting, then moving on to the next. Curious about who the artist is, the title of the painting, and the date, and even what the price might be, you likely spend more time squinting at the label posted on the wall beside the painting than what you purportedly came to see!

There is another familiar way of not-looking, which is being distracted by all the baggage we bring into the gallery with us—often even without knowing that we brought it. This is the history of our likes and dislikes, prejudices, everything we think we "know." Everyone knows what "art" is, and perhaps especially what it's NOT! Abstract art, some think? My child could do it! Landscapes? Portraits? Passé, old-fashioned, 19th century, of no interest today. Installation? Conceptual art? A con job. Even painting itself was pronounced dead just a few decades ago. These received ideas and prejudices are so powerful they can blind us, and we end up looking at what we *think* we see instead of what is actually on the wall in front of our eyes. I know this is true because I have caught myself doing exactly this—and then going home to write a review!

It was no coincidence, I suspect, that I stumbled into meditation around the same time I began to think about *not looking* at art. Meditation was something I had often thought about but had always scoffed at, thinking myself too busy in my head. When I was encouraged to start out tentatively with ten minutes, fifteen minutes at a time, I tried it out and was quite pleased with myself. But then I heard about a sitting group that met in my neighborhood and called to inquire about it. The meetings began, I heard, by sitting for an hour, before a second hour devoted to discussion. A whole hour! Impossible! But I was tempted. I tried. I sat. For that first whole hour. And miraculously, contrary to my expectations, I did not expire from boredom or frustration. Or from the agony of sitting still. In fact, I felt pretty much elated by my grand achievement.

It was not long after that I started thinking: one hour, one painting. Why not? I tried it for myself, sitting in front of a single painting for an hour. Just looking. Without judgment. Without "knowledge." Just sitting, *not-thinking*, and looking at what was there on the wall in front of me. For an hour.

That was twenty-five years ago. I have been doing it ever since. I've done it dozens of times, by myself as well as with groups of others, in a series of events I began offering in museums and galleries, and even on occasion in private homes. I came up with a name for the sessions: "One Hour/One Painting."

The first thing I ask of participants is to put aside the baggage they brought in with them—the likes and dislikes, the assumptions about what good art looks like, and what is bad. Then I give a little basic introduction to the meditation practice and we do a little closed-eye work, concentrating exclusively on the breath and emptying out the passing thoughts, the prejudices, the distractions. Then we open our eyes and gaze without judgment at the surface of the painting that I've chosen. Some of my guests already love it before we start to look at it. Others hate it. I myself can love or hate it. It doesn't matter. What matters is that we simply rest our eyes on it, moving through its surfaces in total concentration, asking it only to reveal itself to our gaze. Leading the process, I don't lecture my group about the painting or attempt to explain it. I walk them through it, bringing them back and forth between moments of closed-eye breathing meditation and moments of open-eyed contemplation and awareness, drawing their attention to different passages here and there, to the qualities of shape and color, the surface texture. It's a matter of just looking, restful and attentive all at once, allowing the painting to simply be itself. As the artist Frank Stella put it: What you see is what you see.

I invite opinions only at the end. In the last ten minutes of the hour, we talk. Most people—those who have never experienced meditation—are eager to comment on how relaxed they feel, and how refreshed. Some want to talk about the newness of experience itself, others about the painting, and whether they like it more, having looked at it so attentively for so long, or less. I ask myself the same. Sometimes my first reaction is unchanged: I still love the painting, perhaps even more than when we started; or I'm still not keen. But at least we have all given it the chance to be what it is, not what we expect it, or tell it, or assume it to be.

So there is an art involved in looking at a painting—although "skill" may be the better word, because a skill can be honed, as can the art of meditation. It's a matter of practice, focus and attention. It requires no special ability, no special quality of mind. We all have busy ones. But we live in an age of intensity and unremitting speed where it's a blessing to be able to stand back and train the mind not to follow its own often unhelpful side trips, but instead to do what comes only with discipline and practice: to wake up and pay attention.

Ekphrasis

I first came upon the word *ekphrasis* when I was contacted—along with several other writers—by the Dutch painter Gerrit Joost de Jong, requesting a response to one of his paintings in the form of a poem. I complied, initially with some misgivings. I had been writing *about* art professionally for many years, as a "critic"—I always put that word in quotation marks, because I never felt like one—but this was a different challenge: to create a work of language art in response to a work of visual art. An act of translation, or interpretation from one medium to another; but then not yet quite interpretation, more of a reimagining in a different creative language. An act of homage, too.

I recall my work long ago as a translator of poetry from other languages into English. "*Better a live sparrow*"—so Edward Fitzgerald said, in reference to his classic translation of the Rubaiyat of Omar Khayyam—"*than a stuffed eagle.*" The metaphor invokes the creative reaction of one artist/writer to the inspiration of another. I recalled, too, the origins of my own journey from poet to art critic back in the 1970s, in the early days of what was being referred to as conceptual art. I went to a gallery expecting to see paintings on the wall and left appalled by what appeared to me nothing but a disgraceful mess of badly assembled mixed media. My response was already ekphrastic—a thirty-page poem that attempted to come to terms with what I'd seen. In a very real sense, I have always thought of my critical writing as poetry, which may explain why I'm uncomfortable with being called a critic.

Just recently I had the good fortune to see a new off-Broadway play in New York called "The Thin Place." The "thin place" of the title, as I understood it, was the membrane that separates our individual experience of the world from that of every other human being. Stretched thin, it invites a quasi-telepathic communication between one sphere of reality and the next. Understood in this way, it is perhaps the thin place that we're given to explore in the act of ekphrasis. We recognize a fellow spirit who seeks to communicate with us in the form of a poem, a painting, to tell us something of who they are. Something vital. Something urgent. We "hear" what they're trying to say and recognize something of ourselves. And try, then, in return, to tell that person something of ourselves.

Ekphrasis, it seems to me, is an act of love. It's a profound "I see you" and "You see me" experience. Or what the philosopher Martin Buber memorably called "I-Thou." It's a celebration of our common humanity and, at the same time, a tribute to our irreducible individuality, an attempt to reach through the thin place that separates us to bring a fellow human being into the warmth of our embrace.

Prejudice

I have been going through a box of family memorabilia—photographs, invoices, documents, certificates... And letters. Lots of letters. Some insignificant, many illegible, many others whose relevance has been lost in the intervening years. And here and there I find letters that startle or shock, or move me for their sincerity, urgency, compassion.

Amongst all this, I found a letter written by my favorite uncle Neil to Harry and Peggy, my parents, back in 1960. It was written from what was then still called Rhodesia, where he had made his home. He still identified himself as a "European" while his children, he wrote, were Rhodesian in every way. It was their home. They could not imagine any other. My uncle Neil, as I knew him, was a handsome, carefree chap. He was reputed in the family to be a bit of a rogue, and perhaps this was why he was the favorite uncle of a boy growing up in the restrained circumstance of an English country village and private school. He was—scandalously, in those days of social propriety—divorced from his first wife and had remarried. When he came home to England to visit on occasion, he stood out from the rest of us pale islanders with features tanned by the African sun and a big, sunny grin that was a rare sight amidst the usual aspect of English faces rendered dour not only by the recent experience of war but also, surely, by the gloomy weather that graced our little island. To this little boy my uncle seemed a joyful, unabashedly libertine presence in our midst.

So here's my favorite memory of my favorite uncle. At "prep school"—a boarding school for boys between seven and twelve years old, I was always a bit shy, never a good mixer. I felt like a prisoner in the big old Georgian mansion that housed us. I did not know, I'm sure, what it was I longed for with such desperation, but in retrospect I'm pretty sure that it was freedom. We boys were there for three trimesters every year, autumn, spring and summer, and those periods of captivity seemed interminable. If we were lucky, our parents might come down at half term to "take us out." My own parents, "Mummy and Daddy" as I called them, would come down once in a rare while, take a room at a local inn and fetch me from school to spend an afternoon with them in the inn's beautiful green garden. If the sun shone, we would sit outside and indulge in the rare treat of strawberries and cream, with a dash of sugar on top for crunch. I can still taste them. When my 12-year-old grandson comes to stay with us, I never fail to prepare this same treat for him at breakfast time.

Imagine my delight, then, to hear that my favorite uncle was coming to take me out! Imagine the sheer elation of this little boy in his gray school uniform, seeing his favorite uncle speed up the long drive to the school in a stylish sporty convertible with the top down, basking in the knowledge that this spectacle would ignite envy in the heart of all his classmates! I climbed into the car beside my glamorous uncle, prouder than I had ever felt in my life before, as we drove off together, just the two of us, in bright Sussex sunshine. We meandered along country roads for a while, as I recall, with the gentle green slopes of the Downs rising up on either side. Perhaps we stopped somewhere along the route for tea and biscuits or iced cake.

But the best part still awaited. Long before motorways were dreamed of in my native country, there was the new marvel that was called a "dual carriageway"—modeled, I'm embarrassed to suspect, on the

"Autobahns" built in Hitler's Germany in the 1930s. Beginning to replace some of the so-called "A" roads, these were wide, open highways, with one-way traffic on each side and a grass border in between. There happened to be one not far from my school, just a few smooth miles with traffic so sparse there was virtually no other vehicle in sight. As he ventured forth in this irresistible temptation, my Uncle Neil's blue eyes gleamed with daring. He stepped down on the accelerator and the convertible powered forward. My uncle turned to me briefly with a devilish smile (do I remember or am I imagining a bright scarf at his neck, flying out in the wind?) and shoved his foot down further. Within moments we were speeding faster than I'd ever driven before, much faster than my father ever dared to drive, faster than I ever thought possible. Seventy, eighty miles an hour... Thrilled, terrified (there was no such thing as a seat belt in those days) I watched the needle jerk up on the speedometer. Ninety, ninety-five, a hundred miles an hour! A hundred miles an hour! My uncle was grinning in triumph, happy to be showing off and loving the thrill of it just as much as I did. All too soon, though, he had to ease his foot off the accelerator again, braking hard, and returning to a safer speed as we approached the end of the short stretch of dual carriageway.

So here was an uncle I could boast about! Here was a story I could take back to astound everyone at school. The memory is among my happiest of childhood.

It was many years later that I read his letter to my parents, and that whole generation had long since died. It was written at a time when former British colonies like Rhodesia were under increasing pressure from African nationalists who were fighting to take their countries back. The old colonials still clung to the long-held conviction in the innate superiority of white European settlers, their right to rule, and their Christian obligation to rescue Black Africans from pagan ignorance and savagery. My uncle's letter—

long, impassioned, righteous—expressed his outrage at the British government for abandoning its responsibility to support the old Empire, along with his love and understanding of the African people. They required either a good thrashing—his word, my favorite uncle's!—or a gift to remind them that a promise must be kept. The indigenous Rhodesians, in his letter, appeared as simple-minded children who, if given the freedom they demanded, would soon resort to their natural barbarity. He cited the Congo, then in the grips of a great upheaval, as evidence of the violence of which Africans were capable when given their freedom.

At some deep, conveniently secret place in my consciousness, I know that I carry my own share of the white man's heritage, and that this shameful prejudice and fear of the "other" persists in our culture here in America today, arising in subtle and not-so-subtle ways. The "great replacement" theory that drives the darkest behavior in American social and political life today is an expression of that same hidden prejudice and fear. It is my work, and the work of everyone with a human conscience and a clear sense of what is right, to put the arrogance and inhumanity of the past behind us. I like to think that my favorite uncle, were he alive today as a man of intelligence and conscience, would have repudiated the kind of thinking that properly belongs in the past, and would have wished for no less.

Past And Future

One good reason to follow a meditation practice is to teach the mind to learn to stay focused in the present moment. When the mind wanders off, as it likes to do, it is inevitably in one of two directions: past or future. While this can produce pleasurable results in the form of a stirring memory or the anticipation of a joyful event to come, it is often accompanied by anxiety or stress: did I do this right, did I do enough, did I do it well enough? Or what should I say and how should I say it? What must I do to get what I want? How will that critical meeting turn out? And so on. The mind is always busy creating stress, anxiety, doubt, regret, anticipation—all of which add up to suffering.

Conversely, though this is not to say that the mind can't also be usefully critical of what is already competed; or creative, imagining new projects yet to be completed, original images, stories or poems to be written. We are admonished to live in the present, but does this preclude invention, discrimination, striving?

Damn. Just one more conundrum.

Overpopulation

I can't help but think that most of our social and political problems can be attributed to one vexing cause: there are simply too many of us on this poor old planet. Everyone is afraid, everyone is oppressed by the sheer numbers of our fellow human beings, everyone worried that what they have—whether much or little—is at risk of being taken from them. Our climate problems are driven largely by the need to provide us all with power—power to heat and cool, power to drive our engines and our industries, power to make the things we need and ship them to the places they are needed. Still dependent on fossil fuels to supply that power, we know that burning fossil fuels is the cause of further damage to our already compromised environment. In all this, people are driven from their homes by violence, disease and hunger, desperately seeking asylum where existing populations reject them, fearing the impact on their own lives.

The political consequence is a return to strong-arm fascism and renewed faith in the false promises of politicians who have loud voices but no ability or intention to fulfill them. We have Giorgia Meloni in Italy, the short-lived Liz Truss in the UK, Viktor Orban in Hungary. We have surging right-wing movements in France, in Germany, in the Netherlands, in Sweden of all places! Here in America, we have Trump and MAGA and the very real threat of recalcitrant gridlock in Congress. Empowered for now, Republicans have no policies to resolve the problems that we face and conspire to choose instead to bicker among themselves and attack anyone with whom they disagree. The needs of the poor, the destitute, the hungry, and the sick are increasingly ignored, as government programs to provide aid are slashed to provide tax cuts for corporations and the very rich.

One means to address this overarching problem may be to increase global access to birth control—a means devoutly opposed by male-dominated religious powers throughout the world, including here in America. With ignorance, poverty, and the subjugation of women to the will of male supremacists desperately clinging to the power they once had, populations will continue to explode in areas that can least afford to maintain them. In desperation, people will continue to be forced to seize the option of migration, and the instability between nations will continue to rise.

Failing common agreement among human beings to address these challenges to the future of our species, it will take a cataclysm to ensure minimal survival in a greatly diminished future: a global nuclear war, for example, with mass loss of life; a new and less manageable pandemic; or the collapse of the natural infrastructure and the destruction of a vast swath of humanity.

The only thing that is left to us, at least for the immediate future, is the vote. In coming elections, we must vote with careful consideration for the consequences of our choices. We must vote against the cynical, the obstructionists, the power-hungry, and politicians in denial of basic, incontestable facts. We must vote for reason and sanity, compassion, good will and good conscience. Here in America, today, the choices confronting us could not be any clearer.

Always Before

Always before boarding school, it was boys and girls. It was Charles and Caroline. It was Elizabeth, whose father was in the RAF. It was Hillary, from down by the pub. It was Robert John. It was Michael. It was Flora and me. This was the Rectory school, and the war was on. My father, the skilled carpenter, made us blue and yellow boxes, big enough for all your books and pencils, big enough to use as stools to sit on.

And then, come time to leave for boarding school, it was the trip to Gorringes, the London department store, to buy the school uniform, grey jacket and shorts, black and white knit tie, socks also trimmed in black and white. The school cap, black with white stripes coming out from the center. The Blitz was over by now, but the war was still raging on the Continent. In London, there were still sandbags everywhere, piled in front of entrances to buildings. There were sentries everywhere, too, eyes alert, with rifles and tin helmets. But the taxis were out on the streets again, and bright red double-decker buses.

After that, it was all boys. It was Euston Station and the railway train all the way north to Ambleside in the Lake District, where the school was evacuated for the war. All the boys were dressed in the same uniform, grey, with black and white stripes. There were painted black and white bands at each end of the trunk where your mother packed all your clothes, and black and white bands around each end of your tuck box loaded with treats she sent with you. Slices of fruit cake, jam jars, biscuits…

Euston Station. The smell of oil, of grease on metal, the smell of hot steam, and coal smoke from the engines. The clatter of porters scurrying everywhere with carts piled high with trunks and suitcases. The hiss of steam, the scream of brakes, the goodbye shouts, the whistles as the train got the signal for departure. The slow grind of steel wheels on steel rails at the start of the long journey. The clamor of boys at carriage windows, waving their last goodbyes to parents left standing on the platform, waving back.

In the carriage, there were boys everywhere, fighting for seats, greeting old friends, yelling insults at old enemies. Boys of seven, like myself, and older boys of ten, eleven, twelve. No first names now. No Peter. I am just Clothier. There are dozens of others, Massingbird-Mundy, Fitch, Hopkinson, too many to remember.

The rain pulls away from the station and picks up speed through the London suburbs, and we size each other up, on the watch for future friends but mostly finding those to beware of. Boys who are bigger, stronger, smarter. Boys strutting and smirking confidently up and down the corridor. Boys sucking on lollipops or tearing wrappers from a Cadbury's chocolate bar. Boys rapt in comic books, boys boasting of their holiday adventures. Boys…

There was no more before. From now on everything was after. You had to learn to live with it.

The Magic Flute

We went to the Metropolitan Opera, Ellie and I. Not in New York, of course, but relayed live in a movie theater. We had been hearing about these streamed performances for a while already, but this was the first time we acted on the opportunity—and this time largely because our friends had mentioned it at dinner the night before and invited us to join them. The chance to see "Die Zauberflöte" seemed too good to miss.

Our friends were better advised and forewarned by previous experience. Having checked the start time on the theater's site online we arrived promptly at the advertised 9:30 in the morning—a good Englishman, I am constitutionally unable to arrive even a minute late, a constant annoyance and embarrassment to my California wife, who has long abided by the local custom of arriving properly late—and parked in what turned out to be the wrong parking lot, absurdly expensive and too far from the theater. Our more experienced friends knew where to park and had relied on the more accurate 10:00 AM start time advertised in the Met schedule. The theater had required our early arrival, it seemed, in order to regale us with a full 45 minutes of commercials for various products and countless future events before the curtain finally went up at 10:15. I thought it lucky that Mozart could still make magic with his music because I was frankly ready to get up and leave before the overture!

Still, there it was, displayed on the giant screen: The Magic Flute. As surely intended by the composer, the overture already shook me out of my stupor, and the opening scenes were as enchanting as only Mozart can be. You can't beat that. And this, we decided after settling in, is a good way to see opera. Rather than sitting in costly seats way back in the audience, you find yourself right there in the orchestra pit with the conductor, right there on stage with the performers—I won't call them singers because in camera range this close, there was as much acting required of them as simply giving voice to the arias.

The staging was great—a kind of meta-performance, the cast interacting playfully not only with each other but with both the conductor and different members of the orchestra. The audience, too, was constantly engaged in the events, following the action through the presence of an onstage sound-effects woman in constant "conversation" with the performers, principally Papageno, the piper. a clownish sidekick to the story's hero, Prince Tamino with his magic flute. This audience-friendly acting worked well, and it's barely necessary to add that every one of the voices was superb. The highlight for me--and seemingly also for an enthusiastic live audience in New York--was the haunting aria where the Queen of the Night hands her daughter, Pamina, with a dagger, commanding her to kill the villainous Sarastro.

The plot is incredibly silly. It is based on the male initiation ritual practiced by the order of Freemasons—in which Mozart himself was first an apprentice, then a Fellow (inducted on Ellie's birthday in 1785!), and finally a Master. Before being allowed to consummate his passion for the lovely Pamina, Tamino requires admission to Sarastro's temple, where he submits to the traditional ritual ordeal—through fire, water, etc., etc. Make what you will of the comically, naughtily phallic "magic flute" that is the gold at the end of this hero's journey, the Met's performance plays it up with lusty humor.

Anyway, to nobody's surprise, hero and heroine find their own true love and—to borrow from another master of the stage—all's well that ends well.

So, a lot of fun, and a good way to see opera. I have never been a big fan of either opera or ballet, which are perhaps too esoteric for my simple, practical aesthetic tastes. I remain, as I have often said, an English country village boy at heart, far from a big city sophisticate. But I can always make an exception.

Country Boy

So, yes, I have been thinking about my inner country boy, particularly in light of recent and ongoing online exchanges with a fellow writer who often comments on my social media posts. His barbs are always welcome. He is smart, well-informed, a well-known and nationally published writer who writes what I think of as real art criticism. His work is, unlike my own, truly critical, assessing with reasoned arguments and well-thought aesthetic judgment the difference between the good, the bad, the indifferent. Also an accomplished and dedicated painter, he remains a fiercely unapologetic intellectual—and no disrespect for that! The word "urbane" comes to mind. An exacting rationalist, he delights in poking holes in my every lapse in logic—of which I must admit there is no shortage. He is also an uncompromising atheist, who immediately dismisses any suggestion of religious or spiritual belief as superstitious nonsense.

I am always grateful to someone who challenges my assumptions and asks me to think again. I see myself and this friend (I first omitted that "r" and called him "fiend"!) at opposite poles. As a widely published art writer myself (my readers know that I avoid the appellation "critic"), I was never so rigorous or knowledgeable as he, and the record of my publications is no match for his. I am definitely not urbane. I remain an English country boy at heart. For many years I played the part of an academic and an intellectual—and reasonably successfully so—but I never felt comfortable in that role. Having climbed the educational ladder to the respectable heights of a doctorate, I spent a good number of years in academia before admitting that I never belonged there in the first place. It has been many years since I quit and I have been much happier as what might be called a gentleman of leisure—though I never stopped working, and for the most part harder than I ever worked in academia.

I have come to accept that at my inner core, I nurse the same little boy whose earliest and happiest years were spent as a child in a quiet English country village. It's just who I am. Polite, though sometimes mischievous. A bit simple-minded. A lover of nature, more so than of books, or music, or art. Tending to accept what is for what it is. Less at home in the big city than a village, a little seaside town. Easily awed and lacking, for the most part, in guile or ill-will. Kind of innocent, I suppose. Wide-eyed. No longer a believer in God but certainly in things greater than myself, things invested in meaning that transcends the merely explicable or utile. And willing to blurt out whatever happens to be in my mind at any given moment. As a writer, I see myself in the grand tradition of the amateur, one who simply does it for no other reason than the love of it.

There's a familiar old song with a title that I always liked: "Thank God I'm a country boy." That's me. A country boy. The chorus goes, in part "Life ain't nothin' but a funny, funny riddle." I get that, too; I love riddles. But still, I prefer to be known as an English country boy than an American one—and there's a world of difference between the Appalachians and the soft green hills and meadows of Hertfordshire, where my spirit lives.

Three Boys

We are fortunate to have a lovely young woman helping us out around the house while Ellie recovers from her broken hip, and just yesterday she happened to mention that her family was celebrating the birthday of a younger brother who died of leukemia many years ago, at the age of 15. He would have been 33 today, she told us. Clearly, his memory lives on with her mother and the family, and I thought it touching that they continue to celebrate the day of his birth rather than the day of his death.

Her story put me in mind of two boys in my own family who did not survive into adult life, and of my own brush with death at a very early age. One of the two, a cousin—sadly, I no longer remember his name, it was so long ago—died at the age of five when hit by a bus on a city street. This would have been in the war years or shortly after, because it came at a time when his mother, my aunt, came visiting quite frequently with her other children at the Rectory where we lived, especially at Christmas time when her husband, my uncle, an Anglican priest like my father, was serving abroad as a chaplain in the military. I remember having learned as a child about my cousin's death, but the memory is hazy because it was mentioned only in hushed whispers. (I do remember clearly taking a bath with his older brother—we children shared baths in those days—who shocked my innocent self when he suggested playing shipwreck with his little toy boat. The game required him to raise his butt and poke his penis out from below the sudsy water. This was the lighthouse, and his testicles were the treacherous rocks below. He invited me to do the same, but like a good little boy I knew that it was sinful to play with my penis. So I declined.

The other boy who died was the one who would have been my uncle had he survived, my mother's younger brother. His name was Tony. He died of an infection in the days before penicillin was discovered and saved countless human lives. I know this story because a similar infection could have taken my own life not too many years later. My grandmother happened to be staying with us at the time, and I clearly remember the panic brought on by her terror that I would suffer the same fate as Tony.

It was Christmas time—another detail I recall because the symptoms of the infection started in my leg when I was out with a group of my father's parishioners singing Christmas carols outside houses all around the village. Or was I out with the bellringers? We would ring out the carols in complicated sequences on our handbells with their leather straps, eight of us in a circle, faces glowing in the light of a lamp in the winter darkness. On that occasion I came home limping badly, with rapidly spreading, paralyzing pain in the affected leg, serious enough to call the doctor in the middle of the night as my grandmother insisted. In those days the local doctor would respond immediately with a house call, no matter how late, so Dr. Robertson—I believe that was his name—arrived with his black doctor's bag, the kind that doctors used to carry with them everywhere. He was a kindly, silver-haired man with a bristly mustache who checked my leg, quickly diagnosed an infection, and gave me a shot of the miracle drug, penicillin. Without it, I would likely not be here to write these words. I am quite literally fortunate to still be alive today more than eighty years after that eventful Christmas Eve, even if now headed, frankly, toward the exit. What a privilege to have enjoyed a life well lived, with every one of its pains and joys. Looking back, I'm happy to thank the good Dr. Robertson for having made sure that I didn't miss out on it!

Tragedy or Farce?

It's hard to know whether the worrisome events that are happening in America today would qualify as tragedy or farce. A noted professor of Comparative Literature in my doctoral study days used to argue that farce is the only possible form of tragedy these days. A strict Aristotelian, he dismissed the canon of 20th century social realist drama—the work of Eugene O'Neill, Tennessee Williams, Arthur Miller and so on—as pathos rather than tragedy. Tragedy, he argued, required the presence of the gods to make sense of the universe, whose disruption and restoration were the essence of the tragic vision. Since the gods absconded, we are bereft of their reassuring presence; the world is turned upside down, and in the absurd, meaningless, upside-down world the clown is the true tragic hero. I think of Beckett, Ionesco, Pirandello, the Theater of the Absurd...

Write this off if you will as pretentious lit-crit gobbledy-gook, but I had no trouble seeing the sense in it. It may well be the last time I saw much sense in literary criticism since the invasion (from France, of course!) of the highbrow, turgid critical dogma of our time. Now that I'm old and no longer need to pretend, I can publicly confess that once the practitioners of this critical approach took over—Foucault, Derrida, Lyotard, and the like— my poor befuddled English brain was left lying in the dust. For a while, still in academia and required to teach classes in critical theory, I managed to stay a step or two ahead of my students, making a reasonable show of pretending that it all made sense. I considered myself lucky not to get caught out by the smarter students in my classes. (As an exception, I did connect with Gaston Bachelard and the phenomenologists, whose writing dove-tailed with my own experience and my way of looking at the world).

There I go! My readers today deserve better than intellectual pretension. My justification is that this is a moment in history when we are daily reminded, like it or not, that we live front and center on the stage of Theater of the Absurd, where chaos and slapstick rule, and the clown is king. Or wanna-be king. Also, when it's sorely needed to maintain at least a semblance of sanity, it's not a bad thing to have a good laugh at our pretensions

The Hardest Job

We men must learn to become better fathers—and I say that not least for myself. Too much of the dysfunction in both our personal and our public lives can be traced back to the casual, long-lasting and slow-healing wounds inflicted by uncaring, overly demanding, addicted, or otherwise abusive parents. The responsibilities of fatherhood are awesome, and too many of us are not up to a task that falls on shoulders that are ill-prepared and too often fatally compromised by self-involvement, or ignorance, or both.

There is no training manual for the hardest job most men will face, and too many men run from the burden of that responsibility. Some do so literally, running off with a new and less encumbered partner to what they imagine to be a life of freedom from the burdensome restraints of married life. Some surrender to the demands of work, whether real or self-inflicted. Some distract themselves with the ephemeral delights of sex. Others turn to other addictions: alcohol, drugs, sports, gambling, computer games, pornography ... The attractions are endless. Meanwhile, precious sons and daughters are abandoned, often left to improvise their own substitutes for the absent father. Many are scarred by the consequences, suffering through their later years, and unknowingly inflicting the same suffering on those around them—including, sadly, those who love them and those they love the most, their own children. It's a tragically familiar cycle.

In public life, absent the benefit of having had loving, conscious, and well-grounded fathers, men elevated to positions of power can wreak havoc, as we have witnessed at great cost in recent years. We have seen how deeply wounded, ungrown men lead nations into chaos, into wars that serve no purpose other than to compensate for their sense of inadequacy or resolve their inner conflicts.

In a profoundly troubled modern world, especially, we must learn to become better fathers—fathers to children who will grow up to meet their own responsibilities, moving on from a happy and safe experience of childhood to a responsible adult life, children who have themselves inherited the foundational skills to be better fathers to their daughters and sons.

In the long, painful experience of having inflicted my own personal wounds on those I loved, the hardest lesson I had to learn on my path to greater maturity was that to become a better father I needed first to take a hard look in the mirror and become a better man. Perhaps because our fathers failed to teach us, too many of us know little about manhood. We tend to assume that manhood is first and foremost proved by the exercise of that beguiling piece of flesh that dangles compellingly between our legs, itself the agency of fatherhood. We measure our manhood by its pleasures and conquests. Or we measure it instead by our physical prowess or the power we exercise over other people—the macho syndrome. We measure it by our success in sports, finance or business, our celebrity as artists, media stars, or politicians.

We are mistaken. We fail to understand that manhood is rather a matter of human dignity. Authenticity. Commitment. Passion, and compassion. Decency. Dedication to a life of service. And most of all, integrity.

What is integrity? As I have said in the past, it describes the proper balance—the "integration"—of four human qualities: the intellect, the physical body, the emotions, and the intangible quality of spirit. The intellectual is generally unproblematic for men. It comes to us naturally to live in our heads. We trust in reason. We work things out. We argue. We solve problems. We know best. The physical body also presents us for the most part with few problems, especially when we are young. We are naturally strong and tend to take our physical superiority for granted—especially when it comes to sex! Ask any woman. We have a harder time with emotions. We are not comfortable with them. We learn from a young age that this is where we are most vulnerable: feelings expose us to ridicule, abuse or exploitation. We protect ourselves by hiding them from others as well as from ourselves, failing to understand that if we keep them tamped down inside for years, they may eventually explode—and when they do, it can be in ugly, unsafe ways, endangering those closest to us, especially, culpably, our wives and children.

As for our spiritual needs, having scornfully dispensed with the gods since the Age of Reason, we have been left uprooted from the deepest and most inexplicable longings of our human existence. Believing in nothing apart from ourselves, our brilliant minds, and the reality they create, we cast about for moorings in some supreme power "greater than ourselves," embracing false or ineffectual gods in the hope that they will save us.

To reconnect with healthy manhood, we must do the work needed to restore the integration of head and heart, body and soul, and only when we find the manhood in ourselves will we become the fathers that our children need. It is time that we turn our attention to this work. I have always found it too easy—objectionable, even—to place the blame for all our social woes on men, but we must own our share. We owe it not only to our fellow human beings but to Mother Earth herself, so abused by the greed of unmindful, ambitious men and battered nearly to death by her selfish, ill-mannered, poorly fathered children. It is time for us to step up to healthy, fully integrated manhood. Only then will we learn to take care of our children, and with them to assure a healthy future for our fellow beings and the planet that we share.

Surgery

It was the first Monday in April when I went in for a total hip replacement on the right side. The right hip, the hospital staff kept reminding themselves, and me, insistently, in a kind of mantra—lest a mistake be made and I wake up with a new left hip instead. The nurse said it. The surgical assistant repeated it when he stopped by to visit me in the prep room before surgery. The anesthesiologist said it again, and the surgeon. Right hip.

They marked their target with a felt tip pen, just to be sure.

The last thing I remember after they wheeled me on a gurney through brightly lit, interminable hospital corridors was the circle of green-masked faces gathered above me, and beyond them the bank of dazzling, high-tech operating theater lights suspended from the ceiling. The surgeon checked in with a cheerful good morning and a reassurance that everything was going to be just fine. Right hip, he said, joining in the chorus. And soon the anesthesiologist and a team of merry associates were busy telling the jokes they must have told a hundred times before as they hefted me over on my belly and bared my backside ready for the epidural injection that would numb me from the tailbone down. I even recall joining in with the general merriment, before suddenly recalling...

... nothing. A peremptory, headlong dive into darkness.

Blessed oblivion.

When I returned to my senses, I was back In the recovery room. Everyone seemed pleased to see me, everyone wanted to know how I was feeling. I was feeling dopey, but not unpleasantly so. I felt, in fact, perfectly relaxed. And curious. I had been told they'd have me walking soon after surgery, but first they needed to check up on my vitals, monitor the signs of my recovery, and provide a minimum of sustenance in the form of... what was it? Apple juice? A Graham cracker?

Before I knew it, they had a walker for me, bedside, and helped me slide my legs out, feet down to meet the floor. And it was true, I walked! A miracle! Slowly at first, across the recovery room floor, my backside embarrassingly bare in the gap between the folds of the hospital gown. Soon I was walking with greater confidence, a whole step at a time. Walking! Remarkable!

An hour or so later they sent me home.

So everything was fine. But those first few days I did need help and it fell to Ellie to provide the help I needed. Getting up, sitting down. Getting into bed, and out. Up and down stairs. The simple things, the kind of things you take for granted until one day you realize you need help. It's a humbling experience but an important life lesson, especially with the approach of age. Old age. What else can you say, at 87 years old? What I had always dreaded most was the prospect of needing help, especially with the basics. The intimate functions. I have learned to say this every day among the first words of my meditation practice: May I look after myself with ease.

Ellie is a few years younger than I but taking care of me after surgery was no easy task. For several days I was unable to share the household chores as I usually do—making beds, doing the dishes, acting as sous-chef with the chopping and dicing. These chores all fell to Ellie now, and it's important that I make this point because they began to compromise her normally high level of strength and energy. I suspect that it was in part the demands of those early days following my surgery that led up to the moment, Thursday evening when she disgorged the dinner she had lovingly prepared.

It was the first time in many years she had experienced such a thing. She was distraught, a bit disoriented. I had the presence of mind to find a large kitchen pan, in case there was more to come—and this proved a wise precaution. There was indeed, a second event, as copious as the first.

Having been looked after for the past few days, it was now clear that it was my turn to step up. Forbidden from bending at the hip to a greater than 90-degree angle, I had to find the means to clean the floor and mop up—a feat I'm proud to say I managed adequately while Ellie took care of her ailing self before we hobbled off to bed.

So that was Thursday evening.

Friday morning, Ellie embarked on one of the important daily chores she'd had to take over from me as I recovered: taking the dog out for his morning pee and poop walk. Minutes after she'd left, I heard her stumble back into the house in great distress. My first thought was that she'd had a close encounter with one of the coyotes that roam our neighborhood streets; but no, she was feeling so horribly nauseous and faint, she had to come home before finishing her walk. With the aid of a cane, I managed to complete Jake's walk and came back to find Ellie ashen pale and dizzy—bad enough to insist that she report the symptoms to our family practice doctor.

The sequence of events that followed over the weekend is a bit of a blur, but I do recall that Ellie contacted the doctor—perhaps through our provider's email system—and was told to go in for blood tests, which she must have done that Saturday. It was in this circumstance, with both of us in compromised health and at our most vulnerable when we were hit by a devilishly clever scam.

Read on...

The Scam

It started with an email, addressed to Ellie from a tech company, thanking her for her continuing business and alerting her to a $399.99 debit from her bank account to renew the service for the coming year.

We do have such arrangements with tech companies—with Earthlink, GoDaddy, Constant Contact, for example—in connection with our websites and my erstwhile blogs, so it is not unusual to receive an acknowledgment of this kind. Still, on this occasion, it happened that I did not recognize this particular charge and was curious to know what service she was being charged for. So I called the number.

Huge mistake! The first of many in this whole sad history. What I should have done—as our daughter astutely observed—though a day or so too late—was log in to our bank accounts and credit cards to be sure the purported deduction was in fact a real one. But no, I called the number given in the email to inquire…

The phone was answered by a friendly voice.

There are many "should haves" to this story, and this was the second. Having made the call, I should have been alerted by the immediate response and that friendly male voice. Why was there no automatic system answering the phone? Why no infuriating menus to navigate? No interminable holds? Too good to be true.

The friendly voice understood my concern and conceded, with polite apologies, the possibility of a mistake. He offered to cancel the subscription and refund the fee. I still had no idea what service was provided, so why should I not accept the offer?

I did. The ever-helpful "Jason" continued to express polite concern. (Was it not strange that the name he gave me was that of my younger son? It established a clever bond, its familiarity helping to inspire a trust I might not otherwise have had. Had this, I wondered later, been a part of his research on potential victims of the scam?) He walked me through a lengthy cancellation process. Once again, I "should have" known it was far longer than was needed, but it kept me engaged right up to the moment when he guided me to where I should fill in the amount of the requested refund, suggesting generously that we round out the $399.99 amount to $400. I would save myself a penny!

As soon as I entered the $400 figure, however, an extra pair of zeros were miraculously appended to the total. $400 miraculously became $40,000! A bit condescendingly toward one so clumsy with the keyboard, Jason held me responsible for the error. I must have applied too much pressure to the zero key and held it for too long. Surely, I protested, the mistake could be easily and speedily rectified? Jason did his best. Oh, no, he declared in exasperation after a moment, the refund application process was already in the system, and there was no way to recall it. I had actually received the $40,000 refund! There it was in my account, he said—and performed some technological magic trick to show me. There it was, incontestably, on the computer screen.

I "should have" been alarmed, of course, by the fact that this tech expert could show me the balance of my bank account, but by this time I was thoroughly confused, ashamed of my own incompetence, and anxious to find a way to get their money back to him. I had no wish to be burdened with money that did not belong to me, so my sole purpose now was to find the means to return it, an obsession that immediately distracted me from what would otherwise have been reasonable suspicions.

Urged on by "Jason,"—who now began to insist on keeping me live on my cell phone—I was persuaded to make a trip down to my bank to arrange for a wire transfer to correct the error. The teller at the bank took down the details (the target bank for the return was in Bangkok! Another "should have"!) and clacked away at her own computer terminal. She seemed puzzled by what she saw and excused herself to consult with a manager behind the scenes. She soon returned with apologies, informing me that the wire transfer could not be completed, for reasons she was unable to explain. So far as I knew, I still had their $40,000 in my account and was by now feeling doubly responsible for its return.

Jason's "boss", a "Mr. John"—how could I have been so gullible!-- was now brought into the picture to help solve the problem. They now insisted on at least a good faith down payment, suggesting $2,000 in Target gift cards, which was, they assured me, the most convenient way to transfer cash if the wire transfer failed. They could easily be purchased at any CVS store. By this time a full hour had passed, and I was scheduled to show up for a post-op medical appointment following my recent surgery, so I prevailed upon Ellie to drive me to the hospital and take care of the gift card purchase. On our way to the hospital, though—with Jason still on the phone, anxious for his money—we passed a RiteAid, and thinking this might be a possible alternative, we stopped and dashed in to see if we could purchase the gift cards there.

Wonderful! RiteAid had Target gift cards, up to $500 each. We bought four, but the scanner needed to validate them showed that only two of the four were valid. What to do? I had to leave. My medical appointment, I thought, was only a short walk away (it turned out to be much further than I thought) so I hobbled off on foot with my cane for support, and left Ellie to sort things out with the folks at RiteAid. I learned only later that she'd had to chase all over town, from RiteAid to CVS to BestBuy in her effort to find the cards—while our tormentors kept upping the ante, from $2,000 to $5,000 to $6,000. Ellie was more and more confused as she listened to (rightfully!) suspicious store managers asking why she wanted so much. Prompted by the persistent Jason, who insisted on accompanying her on the cell phone every step of the way, she resorted to the lame explanation that she wanted them as gifts for her grandchildren.

All this proved to be just the start of three days of fraught negotiations. You would think that by now I would have caught on to the scam; but no, I persisted, ignoring the alerts arriving from our credit card companies via cell phone texts and emails. I had been conned into genuinely believing that I had $40,000 that did not belong to me and I was consumed by nothing but the need to return it. Even when our daughter, Sarah, joined the effort to persuade me of the obvious danger, I insisted. I simply could not live with what appeared to be demonstrable evidence that I had this huge amount of someone else's money in my bank account.

Meantime, Ellie finally succeeded in purchasing $6,000 worth of those gift cards. She was persuaded to pass on the numbers of $5,000 worth by scratching to reveal the hidden numbers on the back. This was the amount they had stolen from us to date in cash equivalence. It now became a matter of "re-paying" them the rest. In recognition of the trouble I had already incurred in my efforts to return the money, they were "generous" enough to credit me $500 and round out my remaining obligation to $34,000—a sum I now managed to settle with an online wire transfer, thinking that this would settle the whole miserable business. But the scammers were still not done with me. They knew a good sucker when they found one and started next to alarm me with dire warnings about the possible tax consequences of having so large a sum transferred into my bank account, as well as they into theirs. They estimated we could be assessed as much as $15,000, for which I would certainly be held accountable by the IRS. This problem could be resolved, they told me, if I wired them an additional $15,000—for which I would of course be immediately reimbursed by a wire transfer from their bank. This sleight of hand, they promised, would avert the tax problem they described.

    This time, finally, I mustered just a last ounce of good sense and balked at a request so outrageous that even I could see through it. The light dawned. Furious, I hung up the phone and blocked further calls. Humiliating as it was to admit having fallen for this very elaborate scam, I ran another check of our bank accounts to calculate our losses. I had spared us the additional $15,000 and somehow managed to rescue the $5,000 from the gift card scam. But the $34,500 was gone. In the days and weeks that followed I contacted every possible resource, from the bank to our local police and even the FBI, in the diminishing hope that the thieves could be identified and forced to make reparations. My bank made every effort to help me recover the money, but all the contact information the scammers had given me proved fake. The money was untraceable, withdrawn within minutes after the transfer from the bank (in Bangkok!) where it had been deposited, and shifted who knows where.

    Impossible to describe how foolish I felt. This was the most expensive lesson I'd ever had to pay for, and the only compensation was the vigilance I have learned to practice ever since. A good thing too, because it wasn't long before the same thing happened again, almost exactly as it had as before. The scam arrived in the form of another email, this time from a company I recognized for having done business within the past: the Geek Squad. They wrote to thank me for my business and inform me that my subscription had been renewed by automatic deduction from my bank account to the tune of $395.95. I had no recollection of having subscribed to their service but, forewarned this time, I checked the sender's address on the suspicious email. It was not from the Geek Squad, nor was it from BestBuy. To be doubly sure, I checked my bank account, where I found no record of the deduction. Another phishing expedition, then. I logged in to Google to check on current scams and there it was. The Geek Squad scam.

  I contented myself with sending the email to the junk file. Is there anything else I should have done? I hated the thought of someone else, possibly as un-tech savvy and as gullible as I had been, falling victim to this kind of abuse. I have read of people who lose a lifetime's savings. But I could think of nothing other than to post my story on social media and hope that at least a few friends would read it and take note of the warning. Given the scope and scale of this new, pernicious industry, however, I doubt that it will do much good. The scammers are plentiful, as are potential victims. I am now astute enough to spot the new attacks that come almost every day and either discard or report them. This very morning, I received notice from "PayPal" to let me know that someone had posted the request for a large sum of money from my account and to "call this number" if I needed further information. What a sad phenomenon, and how quintessential a reminder of what a strange new world this is.

Shadow

I spent a while this morning sitting with my shadow because I had been angry with somebody I'm close to.

It's a familiar concept. We all have our light side and our dark, our yin and yang, our animus and anima. Our masculine and feminine. Our polar opposites. We like to hide our shadow because it's not something we're proud of or want to share with others. For myself, the part I like to show is the light side, the part that cares deeply about every other human being. The shadow is his opposite, the one who doesn't give a toss about anyone but himself. The one who's angry, hostile, selfish, inconsiderate, mean... The un-gentle Englishman.

Still, our shadows do tend to pop out at inconvenient moments, especially when the need arises to deflect the shadow that some other person throws at us, provoking our own to come out to play. Projection is the currently acceptable word for it, the simple mechanism by which we react as though our shadow is not ours, but some other person's. I point my finger to show what a nasty guy this other is. It's a neat trick of the mind.

I find it salutary, then, to sit and watch my shadow from time to time. No use trying to expunge or exorcise it. Try losing your actual shadow when you're standing in the sun. The shadow is embedded in the human psyche. Psychotherapy is a popular way to bring it into the light, but no matter how well you come to "understand" it or trace it back to its origin—in childhood, say, or some traumatic event in your life—I'm sorry, you are stuck with it.

As I remind myself again and again, the best way to avoid having it take over is to be vigilant, constantly on the watch for when it's about to make its next appearance—as it will—and I find myself pointing the finger, getting angry or defensive, making judgments: He's so small-minded, I say, or she's so selfish, those people are so greedy. And this is inevitably the time, I remind myself, when I must trot out the mirror one more time and take a good look at what I see there.

The other strategy is to make friends with the shadow. You, "*hypocrite lecteur,*" as the French poet Charles Baudelaire wrote in one of my favorite poems, "*mon semblable, mon frère.*" "You, reader, hypocrite, my mirror image, my brother." (A hideous translation, of course, as are all translations of poetry. But, as I have remarked before, better a live sparrow than a stuffed eagle). I try to recognize that my "brother" is just trying to help, inserting himself into a difficult situation in order to soothe the threatened ego. Instead of resisting his efforts, I have learned to thank him and tell him simply but firmly that I don't need his help right now.

So there you have it: once again this morning my shadow came out to play. My shadow is an angry one, so it was not an easy reunion. But it was good to see him again, shake his hand, have a needed conversation.

Rosh Hashanah

Because we could not go to Rosh Hashanah dinner, Rosh Hashanah dinner kindly came to us. We had been invited for Sunday evening but could not go because of Ellie's various health conditions. So yesterday, Monday evening, our good friends Sharon and Donald arrived at our home bearing the leftovers from the dinner we'd missed.

It was a great party. Sarah and Luka came over to join us. We said the prayers, lit the candles, and celebrated the breaking of the challah by dipping it in honey. We did not go through the entire service as usual, but enough to feel we had marked the occasion with respect. I am not a Jew * (see footnote, below) and Ellie is not especially observant, but in all our years together we have celebrated the most important of the Jewish holy days—whether with her family, with good friends like Sharon and Donald, or by ourselves. As anyone who reads my writing knows, I am also not a believer in any religion, having long since abandoned my father's Christian faith. However, I am moved by traditional rituals of all kinds and acknowledge their importance in our lives. I consider it important for Luka, too, to grow up with respect for traditions such as these, and with some understanding of his Jewish heritage, passed down in matrilineal order from his grandmother and his mother.

So, there we were, six of us around our dining table, good friends for more years together at such ceremonies than we care to count. There was the feast, reheated from the night before, but still tasty: brisket, roast vegetables, quinoa, followed by peach pie and apple crisp with a choice of ice cream or à la mode. A glass of wine, red or white. And genial conversation. Luka took it into his head (he often does this; who knows why?) to dig out the Stanley measure from where he knows we keep it and start measuring everybody's arm.

Melita, our new Philippina caregiver—this was her first full day with us—kept busy helping out. A good Catholic, she must have wondered where she had landed this time, but she took it all in the best of spirits and proved herself as good a sport as she is a caregiver. We have been begging the home care agency for consistent help and hope that this lovely new arrival will now be with us for a good long while. Another blessing.

Much gratitude, then, to our good friends for making this possible. Homebound for much of the time these days, we need the connection. Breaking bread with them was more than a simple pleasure, it was a joy.

* Unless you count the story of my maternal grandmother, recounted elsewhere in these pages. Born an Isaacson, she always insisted that she came from the "non-Jewish Isaacson" family. By matrilineal descent, that would include me. I remain skeptical but would never have dared to contradict this formidable woman while she was alive.

Roses

Our weekend caregiver, Hattie, arrived this morning with three lovely roses, red and pink, for Ellie who continues to need the help. She (Hattie) had been given some herself, she said and wanted to share the gift.

Such a lovely gesture. Hattie is from Honduras and is, surprisingly, not a Catholic as you'd expect from that part of the world, but a Mormon. She and much of her family converted after immigrating to the US some years ago, and she is quite serious about her religion. Each year, she tells us, she hosts a couple of missionaries in training, soon to be sent off to their assigned destination somewhere in the world.

I have always been skeptical of the Mormon faith and what little I know of the culture that surrounds it, but I must acknowledge that my skepticism is based more in ignorance than knowledge. I have vague notions of polygamy, the church-sanctioned suppression of women, odd underwear, missionaries in white shirts knocking unsolicited at doors, and so on. As I have perhaps too frequently noted, anyone familiar with my meandering hodge-podge of mostly unrelated thoughts will know that I am distrustful of virtually all forms of religion. I am aware of too much damage inflicted on vulnerable human beings by male-dominated religious hierarchies. I confess to being especially skeptical of recently invented religions like Mormonism and—arguably not even a religion—Scientology. Brought up a Christian, I am more tolerant of the various denominations of

Christianity, but even then, not uniformly so. I have a particular aversion to the literal-minded, Bible-wielding brands of fundamentalist evangelism whose shameless hypocrisy casts its long, pernicious shadow over our American political life. I also inherit a historical suspicion of what Anglicans my own tradition brand as Roman Catholicism. My father called them "Romans"; though not reluctant about calling himself a Catholic, he would insist on the "Anglo" part of his affiliation to what, over this side of the pond, is called the Episcopalian church—which is a slightly more liberal, anti-papist version of the faith that has flourished in England since the days of that scandalous, overweight, and pope-defying Henry, he of the many wives. ("Divorced, beheaded, died; divorced, beheaded, survived" was how we kept them in their proper order as schoolboys). Catholicism of the Roman kind has had a rocky and at times bloody history in England starting with the Tudors and the Stewarts.

Buddhism, too, has its patriarchal traditions; even today, I believe, monks continue to take precedence over nuns. Some versions of the faith have different gods, saints, and demons (bodhisattvas, devas, and so on), but one can without disrespect regard them as tangential to the core teachings. While most traditional, non-Westernized forms of Buddhism require faith and are therefore religions by definition, the dogma can be practiced without the trappings of faith (see Stephen Batchelor's classic *Buddhism Without Beliefs*) as the foundation of a richer, more compassionate, more directed life. For this reason, I continue to think of myself as an "aspiring Buddhist." If I am to be reborn—and this is the point on which I remain skeptical—I would like to think that a decent life as a human being will be enough to assure reincarnation as something other than a cockroach or a rat. (If I'm to be a dog, I'd much appreciate being one as pampered as our Jake!)

In the meantime, though, I am happy to be grateful to a human being like Hattie, whose religious beliefs, no matter whether I agree with them or not, have led her to devote her life to giving care to others and to spread joy with the gift of flowers.

Ricardo

Our good friend Ricardo stopped by yesterday. He is a hard man to get hold of these days. We have relied on him for the past 20 years to help us out with all those jobs around the house for which my own incompetence disqualifies me—namely, anything that requires the least skill with tools. Electrical work. Plumbing. Hammering in a nail without deforming it, while also protecting my fingers. Cleaning or replacing filters as required. Ricardo even helps Ellie with the garden, knowing how best to find the right plants for the right location and getting them safely in the ground. In short, he is the "compleat" handyman (sic, with a nod to Sir Izaac!), that I never was.

These days Ricardo is in great demand, like any other competent handyman. He first came to our house with the contractor we hired for some remodeling when we moved in, downsizing from our previous hillside home in 2004 when we decided it was a much bigger house than we needed now that the family was beginning to move one. At the time Ricardo was the contractor's go-to sidekick, whenever there was a tricky job to be done. Later, when the contractor was finished with our house and moved on to bigger jobs, we began to call on Ricardo to help us with our handyman jobs, and for years he was quick to answer our calls. But in time, because he's so good at what he does, he began to attract more important clients, wealthy people in the west part of town, Beverly Hills and Bel Air, who could offer him more attractive and obviously much better-paid jobs than we could.

So even though he remains loyal to us as early clients, Ricardo has been harder to reach in recent years. Like many good-hearted, hard-working Mexican immigrants, he has an innate aversion to the word "no". Rather than offend with a "no", he says "yes"—but then he doesn't arrive as promised, and then rarely on time. Or he forgets to follow up on a call he swore he would return. But then he will show up one day, all smiles and apologies, as quick and clever as ever with the jobs we have for him. He has now taken to bringing his teenage son, Luis, along with him as an apprentice. We welcome the addition. Luis has recently done a great job cleaning out accumulated junk from the pond in our Buddha garden—so-called because the Buddha sits at its edge with his beatific smile, and we plan to give him more of the kind of work we have always given to his dad.

It's hard to believe our friend Ricardo is now nearly sixty years old! We still think of him as a mere lad. It's wonderful to know that he has done so well for himself in the intervening years, and we are grateful that he remains loyal to us in his own way, and as time allows. He is as fond of us as we are of him. He is a kind of prodigal son: we keep threatening to disown him when he fails to show up on time (and sends us Beverly Hills-worthy bills!), but we always end up killing the fatted calf for him.

Anyway, this time the jobs were insignificant. The flap on the dog door leading out the balcony had come adrift. The screen on the window high up in Ellie's new walk-in shower had been detached by the installers and not replaced, as had the little gizmo that supports the hand-held shower. Some of the bulbs on the exterior lights needed to be replaced. I might sound pretty pathetic if I can't even change a light bulb, but these were tricky ones, high up. That's my excuse. At my age and with my creaky joints, I am not as safe on a ladder as I used to be, while Ricardo is still as nimble as a goat. I watch him in awe.

So for this visit, he was in and out in a flash. When next we call we know he won't say "no." He'll say "yes", as he always does, and then he won't show up until we succeed in bugging him until he can't stand it anymore. Then he'll be back at the door with apologies and a big smile, and will fix our problems for us with a speed and ease that put me to shame. And then he'll be sure to send us an enormous bill.

Retreat

I was to have attended another retreat yesterday with my good friends from the meditation group that has been my Sunday refuge for more than twenty-five years. We sit together in silence for an hour, then spend a second hour in conversation. We talk about our meditation practice or discuss some aspect of the Buddhist dharma that is at once our user's manual for living a worthwhile life and our guidebook for compassionate relationships with our fellow human beings. We sometimes veer off into social issues, politics, and the problems of the world. And sometimes we just chit-chat. We call ourselves a *sangha* in a loose application of a term more properly used to describe an assembly of Buddhist monks.

Our group has been blessed for all the years of its existence by monthly visits from the teacher I mentioned earlier, Than Geoff, now more correctly Ajahn Geoff, Thanissaro Bhikkhu, abbot of the Metta Forest Monastery in Valley Center. He has been our teacher, spiritual guide, mentor, and dare I say friend, a brilliant scholar, writer and translator, and a man of delightful, often self-deprecating humor. He is also a great storyteller. Well-known not only here in his own native country but throughout the world, he trained for years in Thailand as a Thai Forest monk. It's an honor for us that he continues to visit our modest little group, especially now that he is invited to speak and lead retreats at much more important, worldwide destinations. While laying no claim to being one of his more dedicated acolytes—and there are many—I respect him enormously.

Anything I have learned about Buddhism is thanks to his generous teaching, and any small measure of wisdom I possess as I age, I owe to him.

It was with great sadness, then, that I missed yet another opportunity to attend one of his semi-annual retreats at the home of a friend in Laguna Beach, especially since attendance this time was restricted to just a handful of loyal followers. I am still reluctant to call myself a Buddhist because I'm unable to wholeheartedly embrace religious beliefs of any kind. I find it impossible, for instance, to accept the doctrine of rebirth—though Than Geoff has playfully assured me often enough that it's not a prerequisite. In any event, my hesitation comes with the sad acknowledgment that I still harbor in my heart the yearning for some deeper meaning in life that I learned from my Christian father, and for the sense of belonging to a common faith that believers share. Buddhism simply makes more sense to me than any other religion to which we humans cling to mitigate our fear of death.

We all need refuge, as I see it, especially in difficult times like these. We are just now recovering from the appalling lesson of the recent pandemic and witnessing the frightening resurgence of autocracy in many parts of the world, including our own. I am grateful to have found this one refuge that has provided me for so many years with a reliable source of solace and support. I don't know what I would do without it.

It is Sunday today. In my childhood years, I never missed going to church. These days I sit in meditation, not only on Sunday with my small group but of fellow seekers, but every other day in solitude. It is my way of making a continuing connection with the kind of inner peace that, in that lovely biblical phrase, "passeth all understanding."

A Critic

I am always grateful to people who take the time to follow my meanderings on social media, and especially fond of those who might garner some pleasure and even a few insights from what I write. I am as susceptible to recognition and response as anyone else, and it pleases me to know when I have managed to touch others in some significant way. Every writer writes to communicate with fellow human beings.

I also have my critics, and I'd be a fool not to welcome them as much as those who praise me. From them, I learn to pay more careful attention to my words and am often prompted into second or third thoughts. Among my most frequent critics is one who was born a short hop across the Channel from my native England, and who shares his countrymen's long-standing intellectual disdain for their delusional cousins across the sea. If I don't misrepresent him, he takes the view that the sciences, particularly those that embrace the Darwinian theory of evolution, are sufficient explanation for all human behavior. He scoffs at me when I see it otherwise.

Most recently he took me to task for writing so much about myself. He went so far as to attribute this failing to an inability to leave my childhood behind and instructed me to "leave myself at the door."

I plead guilty. I do write a lot about myself. What may have escaped my friend's attention, though, is that not only do I have a reason for it, but I have distinguished precedents amongst his own compatriots. I won't presume to compare myself to such literary giants as Montaigne and Rousseau (I admit that of the two I infinitely prefer Montaigne), but both of these were insistent on writing about... themselves!

Precedents aside, there is a reason for what my friend points out as a grievous fault. I look in the mirror not out of pure narcissism or because I have failed to grow up, but out of curiosity. I have always wanted to know more about what it means to be a human being and how to be a better one, and the model closest to me, the one I know best, the one most available tor study is... myself! I believe that the closer I get to the truth about my own heart and mind, the more I'll know about the humanity I share with every other human being.

My most recent book was called "Dear Harry: Letters to My Father." With apologies to my French friend, it is of course about myself. I started the project thinking that I wanted to know my deceased father better, but then realized halfway through that what I really wanted was for *him* to know *me* better. Still, mention the title to anyone—well, anyone who is not actually French—and their eyes light up in recognition. Yes, those eyes tell me, I too wish I had known my father better. I too wish to have felt his love in a way I never did. Yes, there are many things I'd wish to say to him if he were still alive.

When you come right down to it, my writing is not about "myself" at all. My hope is that when I hold the mirror up to take a good look at myself, I am looking at the reflection of a man very much like other men—and not too different from women. And that's the point.

Bottoms Up

I have some thoughts about a recently released book by Kerry Howley entitled *Bottoms Up and the Devil Laughs: A Journey Through the Deep State.*

It came to me attention because I happened to run into the author on one of our daily walks around the hill where Ellie and I have lived for over 50 years, up the street from the house where lived for 35 of them. She was just saying goodbye to her delightful family, about to leave for a book promotion event at Prairie Lights, that venerable old bookstore in Iowa City, where she and I—I many years before she—were both attracted by the Iowa Writers Workshop at the University of Iowa. Intrigued by this chance encounter, I sent away for a copy of her book.

My alarm system alerts me when I hear the words "deep state." I still vividly recall Hillary Clinton's remark about what she called the "vast right-wing conspiracy"—an observation that was widely mocked at the time but has been validated by subsequent events. At the other end of the scale, the extreme right-wing trades on the fantasy of a secret, all-powerful cabal—the deep state—to keep their base in a bubble of permanent suspicion and anger at the government. My eyes glaze over with cynical "these-people-will-believe-anything" resignation and I turn my thoughts to something less delusional. Kerry Howley, in her book, has me thinking further about the term, and a lot more seriously.

Persuasively, with guile and sometimes devastating humor, and also with an impressively researched base of information—the kind of thing that used to be known as "facts" and "data"—Howley, a seasoned reporter, guides us through a nightmare underworld where an infinite number "secrets" is stored for all time by governments, foreign and domestic, hostile and supposedly friendly, and by corporate entities who see in them the chance to pad their profits. Much of this secret material stores personal information about us, our lives, our very thoughts, all of which is classified and stored in digital form in remote, virtually impregnable facilities, the dungeons of our modern-day castle keeps, where a simple email or text like "taking my wife to lunch" is sucked irretrievably into the maw of officially classified secrets. Howley is our Virgil on this journey through a modern-day digital inferno, in which we must stop more often than we'd wish to remind ourselves, "Wait, no, this is real. This is actually happening in our world today." Or then to remind ourselves, "Wait, no, this is processed, manipulated, digitally generated stuff that we are deluded into accepting as reality."

Howley introduces us to a handful of real, almost ordinary but in truth extraordinary people who are sucked into this digital maze against their will and at no fault of their own, and become so desperate to escape back into a world of truth that they rebel. Seduced by anything that seems to offer them truthful, trustworthy, solid ground in a nightmare of delusion, they sometimes grasp for truth, like the unfortunate John Lindh, in primitive, authoritarian cults like the Taliban and Al Qaeda. Or they fall instead into futile, idealistic efforts to blow the whistle, like the equally unfortunate Chelsea Manning. Infinitely more powerful than they are, the self-propagating system chews them up and spits them out with callous, mindless, and efficient cruelty. The last third of Howley's book follows the exasperating tale of the young woman improbably named Reality Winner.

A talented linguist employed by the US military, innocent in her altruism and offended by official secrecy laws used to hide shocking truths about our American treatment of those deemed our enemies, up to and including torture, she breaks the code of secrecy, meaning only to air scandalous truth—and with the greater purpose of making the world a better place. The mendacious, malicious treatment she receives at the hands of officialdom both at trial and subsequently during her time in prison will outrage the fair-minded reader. Injustice is too academic a word to describe the horrors this young woman endured.

 I finished reading Howley's book as news came out about the arrest of a man named Jack Teixeira in the most recent leaking scandal. Reports suggest that this 21-year-old with access to classified information foolishly decided to share secrets with a few friends on an obscure online chat site. His reason? Kicks? Self-aggrandizement? Pure boyish mischief? On the face of it, he seems not that much different from Reality Winner, absent her altruistic motives. He rapidly became an easy target for public condemnation, based largely on his misguided obsession with video games, guns, and extreme right-wing propaganda. Foolish, certainly. Reprehensible, for sure. But hardly worthy of his characterization as a ruthless spy, dead set on the betrayal of his country.

 I'm grateful to Howley for having revealed a different and very real *deep state* which, when aroused, can inflict great harm on people who transgress its arcane rules. Once enmeshed in its web, they find themselves trapped in a Kafkaesque world of digital alternate reality from which they struggle mightily to escape. And not all of them are peddling pedophile delusions in the basement of a Washington DC pizza joint.

School Days

So I must have misremembered. We were at our Sunday matinee concert at Disney Hall this week and I was delighted to find two items on the program with names that were personally familiar to me. One was a short piece by Avro Pärt, the beautiful "*Cantus in memoriam* Benjamin Britten", wonderfully performed by the LA Philharmonic; and the other was a long one, Ralph Vaughn Williams's Symphony No. 8. The two pieces reminded me—or rather mis-reminded me, as it turned out—that both Britten and Vaughn Williams had sons who were my contemporaries at Fields House—my teenage "home from home"—at my boarding school, Lancing College, back in the 1950s. But Britten, I was reminded by Wikipedia, was a gay man who had no children. Vaughn Williams also had none.

So I was wrong. Still, the Vaughn Williams I knew at school—a very tall, rather awkward boy, as I recall, with big glasses and blond hair—was certainly related to the composer. And Benjamin Britten was one of a coterie of famous musicians who were frequent visitors during my time there. As a choirboy, I performed in his opera for children, "Noye's Fludde," on the occasion of one of his visits. With Britten also from time to time came Peter Pears, the distinguished tenor, and Margaret Ritchie, the soprano. The boy my memory mistook for Britten's son was almost certainly Edward Piper, son of John Piper and Myfanwy Evans, both artists of considerable note in England in the 1940s and early 1950s. Piper—we knew each other only by surnames, I can't even remember Vaughn Williams's first name—was a slim, tidy boy, as I recall, with a sweet smile. It's curious that I remember their faces so well, more than 70 years later! Edward Piper went on to become an artist like his parents.

If memory failed me with those other two names, I know that I'm right in recalling one other British composer's son at Fields, Kit Lambert, the son of Constant Lambert. I have told Kit's bizarre story before: after leaving school he went with his friend Richard Mason—also from Fields—on a journey up the Amazon, the kind of exploration the British used to be famous for. All went well until he found Mason dead one day, killed by the arrows of an aboriginal tribe and reportedly cannibalized. Later, back in England, Kit became involved in the then-thriving rock music scene. As manager of The Who he instigated, then produced the rock opera "Tommy". He succumbed to the lure of drugs and alcohol, however, and died at an early age from a fall down the stairs in his mother's house in London.

Ah, school days! Old school chums! Well, hardly chums. Mason became head prefect at the school and once caned me—"six of the best"—for having been caught with cigarettes at a local, strictly out-of-bounds pool room. Naughty me. Sadly, I learned nothing from the caning: I kept on smoking cigarettes for the next 30 years before quitting. Not much better, I suppose, than Kit Lambert's drugs and alcohol, but I'm still alive, and poor Kit has been dead for nearly half a century. There's no accounting for the vicissitudes of destiny.

Old Friends

My dear old friend,

Yes, old! Not only in years—we are both now in our eighties—but in the longevity of our friendship. We have known each other since boyhood. I write to thank you for this long friendship but also, and particularly, for the joy you brought into my life so long ago.

I woke last night thinking of you and saw your face, with its wry smile and freckles, saw it so clearly; and then, immediately, the faces of your parents who welcomed me with such warmth and loving care—your mother's beautiful smile, your father's calm and steady presence, his gentle humor; and then your brother Christopher and your little sister Katherine (does she have a K or a C?); even your grandfather! Was it in Aspley Guise our family knew him? Up by the golf course? Or was it in Barcelona? I saw you all last night as clearly as though you had been there beside me. It must mean something special, that I'm able to recall your faces with such clarity.

Then came tumbling into my mind the other memories---the ones that glorious summer imprinted so deeply in my mind. The long train ride from London to Paris, changing there, and on to Barcelona on the night train; the apartment high in the building up the steep slope of Calle Muntaner, the contrast of brilliant, white light and shadow; the streetcars down below; the Ramblas; Caldetas... For some reason I remember two homes there, one a lovely villa on a hillside, far above the town; the other on a heavily shaded lane in the town itself, close beside other houses, just a short walk to the beach. I remember the visiting businessman's Bentley parked outside, the contrast of that wealth with the poverty of the near-naked street kids swarming all around it, their brown bodies covered in dust and grime; that same Bentley clashing with a donkey cart on a too-narrow bridge, sun-drenched vineyards all around, the local farmer heedless of the damage to the car and the outrage of its owner. I have written about all this before and you have corrected some of the memories. I'm sure they have suffered distortion, some of them even invented since those days.

Caldetas! Yes! The incredible heat of the Spanish sun on my pale English skin on the sandy beach. The ice cream. At night, some kind of fiesta, a public square, brightly lit with strings of lights, with people of all kinds, young and old, lovers and hungry young men on the prowl, all joining the circle and holding hands to dance the intricate, elegant Catalan *sardanas*, whose haunting music pervaded the night air. I wish I could still call that music to mind today—though of course, these days, I could simply Google it! The sugar-coated churros from the nearby stand, the sticky fingers. The ice-cold nutty *horchatas de chufa*.

To me, a twelve-year-old English boy inured to the daily drizzle and grey skies of old Blighty, it was all so thrilling, so magical, so enchanting. But the important thing—and I think why that summer left such a lasting memory—was the warmth, not only the degrees Fahrenheit, which must have been considerable—but the warmth of relationships. The love in your family, first and foremost, but by extension the love that I sensed all around me that was somehow embodied in those *sardanas*, people in actual touch with each other, people close and unafraid of closeness, so unlike that stuffy English distance and politeness I grew up with, their emotions closer to the surface, bodies unencumbered—not only of clothes, because of the heat!—but of inhibitions. The acceptance of life in all its teeming, searing, pungent reality.

Of course, I am romanticizing. I am becoming sentimental, an indulgence thankfully permitted at our age. I repeat myself—forgive me! And I recognize a glow around these memories that leaves them blurry at the edges, susceptible to infinite reshaping. But I think I'm understanding now why that summer with your family was to prove such a key part of my developing psyche: it allowed me to catch just a glimpse of a freedom I was able only to breathe in, unconsciously, at that young age: the freedom of the heart. I was a shy and innocent observer, not yet able to understand or benefit from it. It took me many years before I began to realize how much I needed to reconnect with it.

There, I think I've said it. Said it again, of course, and still not quite well enough for my own satisfaction, but better perhaps in some ways than before, and with a clearer understanding of why that summer comes back to me with such clarity.

So, this comes with infinite gratitude for all this, and with love to you and your family.

Your old friend, Peter

Men and Cars

The car dealership business, as we have rediscovered in the past few days, remains a stronghold for gender prejudice. Ellie and are in the market for a new car—unquestionably the last we shall ever want or need to own. We have driven hybrid vehicles since 2004 when we bought our first Toyota Prius, in the belief that we were making a small but significant contribution to the continuing battle to protect the natural environment.

We have driven a succession of hybrids ever since and are perfectly happy with our current 2017 Prius. The decision to trade it in was motivated less by the need for a new car than by aging bodies that make access to a low-slung vehicle problematic. We thought a small SUV might be the answer and after spending some time researching the possibilities online, we settled on a first choice to take a look and test drive.

The particular make of our choice is immaterial, and I have no wish to badmouth one particular brand when I suspect the experience would have been similar elsewhere. I made the initial visit and liked both the car and the salesman well enough to persuade Ellie to join me for a second look. She too loved the car... and then the question of aesthetics arose. Exterior color, trim, interior color, finish, and so on. White, the color Ellie chose—also my first choice—proved unavailable with the interior she wanted, out of stock, and untraceable for hundreds of miles around in the dealership's computers.

Enter the manager. So far, I had been impressed by the absence of the dreaded car dealership pressure. You know what I mean: If you buy this now, today, this very moment I can give you... etcetera. None too subtle, it has a negative effect on both Ellie and myself. Ellie particularly had her heart set on our choice but the manager, enlisting the support of the salesman and the two of them working on me to join their cause, persisted in offering a different color, a different interior, even a different model. There was the not-so-subtle suggestion—nudge, nudge, wink, wink—that the little woman was unqualified to make important decisions such as this one.

Speaking for myself, I would have compromised and sacrificed the unavailable white in favor of a perfectly acceptable silver exterior, but Ellie was clear about what she wanted. She presented the increasingly frustrated manager with a fine lecture on the importance of aesthetic choices in our lives, successfully resisting the argument of masculine *we-know-better*. I take credit for remaining stoutly on her side.

The manager retreated to his office in what was clearly a bit of a huff. The salesman, on the other hand—a nice man and, to his credit, the doting father of a two-year-old daughter—promised that he would continue to do what he could to find the car we wanted, even if it took a month or two. We thanked him, genuinely, and left with the matter unresolved.

Curiously, barely an hour passed before I got a call from the manager, quite pleased with himself. He had found us exactly what we wanted, negotiating an agreement with another dealership. It would take a while, he said, and he would need a deposit to assure good faith, but the car we wanted would be ours. It's remarkable, I thought, how a little persistence pays off in the end—though a good friend I spoke to mocked my gullibility, insisting that this was the oldest trick in the car sales book. Still, kudos to Ellie for knowing what she wanted and refusing to settle for anything different—or less.

The Health Spa
A Dream

We find ourselves at a fancy health spa, where we have come for Ellie to have her head shaved in preparation for some kind of follow-up procedure for her cancer. We have time to enjoy a fancy lunch in the restaurant and take a walk in the gardens—as elegant and formal as those at Versailles or Belvedere, with expansive green lawns, flower beds, stone steps, and statues.

The time for Ellie's appointment arrives. She is very brave about it, very calm; she has done this before. A long slope leads to the escalator that will take her down, and as she steps forwards onto the top step I notice that she has dropped her small toiletry bag. Thinking she might need it, I gather it up and run to the top of the escalator, calling her name and waving the bag. She turns and manages to walk up the downside of the escalator with remarkable ease.

I must have decided to keep her company because the next thing I know we are in a kind of public anteroom, awaiting the call for Ellie's appointment. It comes soon, and we find our way down a short corridor and into the shaving clinic—a huge, empty white space, like a hospital ward, with only one corner devoted to the designated head-shaving area. There are two young women waiting in neat uniforms. Ellie has to disrobe and put on a hospital gown. She hangs her clothes on one of a row of pegs placed there for that purpose.

I watch the shaving begin, awed not only by Ellie's bravery but also by the beautiful shape of her head, which is slowly revealed.

It is time to leave. Ellie goes one way, I another. I have a train to catch at a certain time. Ellie dresses and leaves first, and I now discover to my embarrassment that I must have removed my own tan Dockers pants, along with my underpants and belt, and I start to search for them on the pegs. No luck. The young women are leaving, distant already. I call them for help, but if they hear me, they pay no attention.

I must finally have found my Dockers because now I am headed back through the darkened gardens. I know that I am late for my train—and for the driver who will take me to the station. My cell phone rings somewhere in my clothing; this must be the driver, waiting for me at the appointed pickup spot. I search for my phone, feeling its shape in my pants pocket, and struggle without success to get it out in time before the ringing stops. When I finally manage to extract it, I call back. My driver is sullen and testy because by now I am very late. Finally, on the train, I realize I'm on the line leading north from London to the village where I lived as a child. I have traveled this same route many times before, in this same railway carriage, hearing this same clanking of the wheels…

If You Meet The Buddha

Even though I'm not religious, my thoughts wander frequently into those aspects of our lives that religion, however inadequately, addresses. In that context, I have been thinking about teachers. By that, I don't mean the regular kind who shows up to educate the young, whether in the classroom or in college lecture halls. I have immense regard for them, and I have to say some sympathy. I have worked as a teacher in many arenas. My first teaching job was at an elementary school in London, a part of the teacher training course I took when I was a very young man and thought to make this my career. Later I taught for several years at grammar schools, at a language night school, and eventually at college. I worked for many years before I finally realized that this was not what I was supposed to be doing with my life, and by then I had started teaching at the very highest level, in graduate seminars with doctoral students at university.

I'm not being modest when I say that I was never very good at it. At the start, I had my young man's insecurities for which to compensate. But even after growing out of these, I remained uncomfortable with the notion that as a teacher I was supposed to be in possession of a certain store of knowledge that was important to pass on to those who lacked it and needed my superior wisdom. Something inside me rebelled against what felt like the pure presumptuousness of that idea. Instead, when I did finally become a halfway decent teacher, I had learned a way to engage in Socratic dialogue with just a handful of students, some of whom remain friends to this day.

I am not referring to that kind of teaching, then, though the early difficulties I describe might arise from a reticence which may be nothing other than a form of pride. No, I have been thinking about another kind of pride, the kind that rejects the act of faith required in submitting to a religious teacher—in my case in the Buddhist tradition, where the relationship is seen as a sacred bond between teacher and student. While not unquestioning—questions, after all, are the foundation of all learning—that bond is a total commitment that requires the surrender of the student's personal ego to the wisdom and training of the master.

It's my understanding that this is the first and necessary step to becoming a true Buddhist, and my inability to take it has left me with a sense of inadequacy and shame. It is not the least of reasons for my reluctance to even think of myself as a Buddhist, which I might otherwise do. I have met several teachers along the path—well, three of particular significance—who have guided me in important ways in my own practice and for whom I have nothing but the deepest respect and gratitude. But I have not been able to embrace any one of them as "my teacher" in the way that I describe. I have never been tempted, like my Fisherman namesake, to cast aside my nets and follow any one leader, not even if he walks on water—though none of them, to my knowledge, have achieved that feat! When all is done, I return to that old Zen koan, "If you meet the Buddha along the path, kill him." Which I take to mean simply that I must do the work myself.

I have given this puzzle a lot of thought, not only recently but in years past. I have wondered whether my reluctance stems from early, formative experiences. Is it because my father was a religious teacher, an Anglican priest who had his own tormented relationship with God? Does my distrust result from having been sexually abused by a teacher as a child? I have to say that these personal considerations seem at best tenuous to me now, from the perspective of some eighty years of age. Perhaps my hesitation is no more than a deplorable kind of arrogance, a refusal to surrender my ever-important self into the hands of a person I judge to be no less human than myself, no less susceptible to human weakness, wickedness, and error.

These recurrent thoughts were revived as I read *The Magic of Vajrayana* by Ken McLeod, a teacher whose earlier books made an enormous contribution to my growth as I started out on this journey. I had reviewed his book *Wake Up to Your Life* for the Los Angeles Times many years before. As its title suggests, it was an exacting wake-up call, and one that reached deep into my psyche. Later, at Ken's invitation, I wrote an introduction for *An Arrow to the Heart*. This latest book is a profound, engaging, and once again intellectually challenging read. What makes it also a compelling read is that it reflects the authenticity of years of personal immersion in the practice and years of thought and study. It is not a book for everyone, but for those interested and committed enough to put in the work that it requires of its readers, it is richly rewarding, an invitation into a world beyond the self and into the more profound realities of life and death.

Once again, I learned immeasurably from Ken's wisdom and experience, but I have been unable to throw myself at his, or any other teacher's feet. While I have my own judgments about the kind of smorgasbord approach I have adopted, I have come to accept that this will continue to be my way—if only because at least it is my own.

My Rage

Dear Greg,

    I woke very early this morning with thoughts about the shock and outrage you experienced on reading the passage in my book, *Dear Harry*, where I confess to having once slapped the woman I loved. It was not the only slap, as you'll recall from the book. Before Ellie, there was Susan. Two slaps. Even now, more than fifty years later, I have no excuses and still feel the shame. But I have reached what you might call an understanding and a forgiveness for that which I cannot undo.

    Perhaps in part because of that slap, Ellie sometimes tells me that my resource of hidden anger continues to inspire in her an element of fear. She is right. It took me many years to recognize that this fearsome monster has been curled up deep inside me since childhood days. Call it anger. Call it rage. What arouses this monster? It can be anything that threatens to invade my sacred personal territory; anything, particularly, that threatens to belittle me or leave me looking foolish; anything my poor vulnerable ego perceives to be an insult; or anything that exposes what I fear to be my weakness to the world.

    An analyst might deduce—perhaps rightly so—that this monster was born when I was separated from my parents as a little boy, sent off to fend for myself in the alien and dangerous environment of boys' boarding school. The monster who still lives on today made his first vividly recalled appearance, also described in *Dear Harry*, in a fight with a boy named Fitch when I was seven or eight years old. I clearly remember the conflagration of that impotent rage. Fitch won. I lost.

I have come to distrust such easy explanations, though, as overly reductive, and too simple to account for the infinite complexity of our actions. My rage is what I described... and more. It is greater than I can understand and more powerful than any explanation a therapist can bring out into the open; nor is it ever subject to surgical removal. He lives on, this monster. I have had the opportunity to confront him face-to-face and have worked hard to learn to live with him on manageable terms. Still, I know that I will never fully appease him, and certainly never slay him with the sword.

All of which is good to know. The vital key to living with this monster is awareness. I'm generally able to tame the beast by simply acknowledging his presence and paying proper heed to the familiar growl when he's provoked. The best thing, I have learned, is to appreciate his good, though usually misguided intentions and make friends with him. He is a stalwart warrior, a watchful protector against all enemies, real or imagined. When brought over to my side he can be a powerful ally.

None of this excuses the slap that offended you, my friend. I know. Slap is a fine word harmless in itself but nicely onomatopoeic in its evocation of the gesture and sound that it describes. I read a poem long ago whose first line went: "So saying she slapped me hard across the face." I think I have the words exactly unless I misremember, and it was "he" who did the slapping and "her" at the receiving end—a trick of memory that leaves me conveniently off the hook! The line caught my attention, though, and obviously has stuck with me this long for a reason. Perhaps it serves to reawaken my sense of guilt and my intention to do better. As one who loves words and spends his life dancing with them, I respect their resonance with personal experience.

So I understand your outrage, Greg, and thank you for having written to me about it. Would I be remiss, however, in holding up the mirror and inviting you to consider the possibility that, in triggering your outrage, my words touched some part of yourself that you might not want to acknowledge? I ask because I have come to understand that when something or someone provokes me to such an intense response, there is usually something that I need to learn about myself.

In any case, I hope to be forgiven for these acts committed long ago and to remain your lasting friend, Peter

Two Dreams

I had two dreams.

In the first dream, I am on a college campus somewhere. I have been found guilty by some academic authority (dean? provost?) of stealing $400 and sentenced to death. Seriously. This is not a joke. I'm terrified. I beg everyone I know—and everyone I meet—to advocate for me, but no one seems willing. I tried to persuade someone who I thought could help, insisting that I did not need to steal the $400. I already have $500 of my own money in my shirt pocket, look, here... I show it, just to prove it. It seems that the authorities remain unmoved. There is nothing I can do to convince them of my innocence...

I wake up, go to the bathroom, and return to bed.

In the second dream, I am at a house in some eastern European city, perhaps in Poland. I have been invited to participate in a kind of theatrical event, but have no idea what my role will be, nor do I know any of the lines. We wait for what seems like a long time before my host informs me that he must go, leaving me in charge of everything. Participants begin to arrive higgledy-piggledy, all very late, outrageously histrionic Thespians all, with no apparent sense of haste. They seem to know each other and sit around a long table in groups, all engaged in loud gossip in their language, which of course I do not understand.

The one instruction I was given by our host, as he was leaving, was to start the event by hushing everyone up. He tells me that to do this I must yell, *Shut the fuck up!* in a very loud voice. I try yelling the words: Shut the fuck up! but at first, no one pays the slightest attention. The chattering continues, even louder. I try again: Shut the fuck up! yelling now at the top of my voice. This time I have their attention. But no one knows what play we are supposed to perform, no one knows what part they are to play, no one knows their lines.

I decide to start the evening with introductions. It now appears that Ellie is here, sitting calmly at the table, already magnificently costumed—though it's unclear for what part. I introduce her to the company. I also introduce myself, but now have no idea where to go from here. What is the play? Is it that Shakespeare drama whose title no actor dares to mention? Alas, the mystery remains unresolved...

Charlie

My friend the artist Ulysses Jenkins was kind enough to send me a copy of a videotape he made back in 1977 at the opening of a Charles White retrospective at the Los Angeles Municipal Gallery in Barnsdall Park. I was tickled to see images of any number of old friends in their younger days—Josine Ianco-Starrels, Betye Saar, Ben Horowitz of the Heritage Gallery, Kent Twitchell—and even a catch glimpse of Ellie and my younger self as Dean of what was then Otis Art Institute. There were also several familiar faces of students from Charlie's drawing class, but I could not put names to them after all these years.

As I wrote in my note of thanks to Ulysses, the video is an absolute treasure. More even than the pleasure of seeing old friends, the segments showing Charlie talking informally to his students in class and at the microphone at the opening of his retrospective were a compelling reminder of his passion and commitment to his work. I went back over the tape to copy down a few words that spoke to me with special resonance about the reason that impelled him to make art: "I needed," he said, "to have this very personal part of me, my gut, my heart, my soul be shared by other people, others outside myself, to begin to find the answers to these questions: Who am I, what am I, why…?"

His words brought me back to the images created by Charles White, the artist, whether of celebrities from among his contemporaries like Harry Belafonte, Sidney Poitier, and Rosa Parks, or great figures from Black history: Sojourner Truth, Harriet Tubman, Frederick Douglass, W. E. B. Du Bois. Whether great heroes like these, or lesser-known figures of his personal acquaintance, or figures dreamed up in his imagination, every one of the people he so powerfully evoked in his drawings is a projection of the self he was driven to share. Man, woman and child, they are all in some way images of Charlie, the man, who so passionately wanted to tell the story and celebrate the power and beauty of Black America through its people.

I was privileged to know Charlie well. We shared many lunches—and many martinis!—at the tavern across the street from the Otis campus, where conversation always competed, even at lunchtime, with a boisterous mariachi band. More importantly, I spent many hours with him in the months before his death, recording long conversations on a cheap tape recorder. The tapes are fortunately now preserved in the Charles White archive, used by scholars, and I hope kept in good condition for the future. Thanks to a Rockefeller Foundation fellowship that funded my research for a year, I wrote a full-length monograph on Charlie's life and work. Completed, the book was turned down by several art publication houses on the grounds that it did not have sufficient appeal to the wider public.

Which is as it may be. The book may not have had the commercial appeal that publishers were looking for. But the unspoken truth, I suspect, is that racial prejudice continued to dominate the art world even as recently as the early 1980s. We are still not free of it today, but it is encouraging that artists of color are increasingly given deserved, often long-postponed recognition in exhibitions in galleries and museums. I hope that my manuscript is preserved in the archive and that what I wrote many years ago will contribute to Charlie's legacy. Frequently passed over by a powerful and commercially driven mainstream in his lifetime, his images have begun to find a proper place in the history of American art, witness the major exhibition that recently traveled to several leading national museums, starting with New York's august Museum of Modern Art. Their value has even recently been validated by the institutional mecca of our capitalist American values, the marketplace, where his auction prices have soared. None of which makes a scrap of difference to his contribution as an artist, a man of great integrity, and a teacher who inspired countless students on the path to recognition and success. Charles White's legacy is assured. I am privileged to have known and worked with him, and to have been one amongst the army of his friends.

Hats Off

I have a score of them. Hats. Brown ones, black ones, grey ones, green ones, blue ones. Hard and soft hats, floppy hats. Expensive ones and cheap ones. I have a fine black Stetson with silver trimmings on its band, an elegant straw Panama, and any number of soft felt hats, each with its own distinctive decorative band, some with jaunty, colorful feathers to jazz them up. Broad rims, narrow rims, all kinds.

I recall precisely when I bought my first hat. I was seventeen years old, anxious to look like a real man of the world. I bought a grey trilby to wear on the way to work at my first job, packing goods for shipping at Gorringes department store in London. But it was only later in life, in my fifties, that I got serious about hats. My hair began to turn grey, and I allowed it to grow long, eventually taming it with a stretchy band into the ponytail by which I was known, along with the hats, for a good number of years. I bought the first of those hats—historically, of course, the second—for a purely practical purpose: to keep the unruly strands of hair from blowing into my eyes. But I soon became addicted. Everywhere I traveled, I would find a new hat to buy, amassing an impressive collection that even today adorns the hallway racks.

But I rarely wear a hat these days. The ponytail is long gone and my hair, once salt-and-pepper but now a complete silver monochrome, is short, and no longer needs restraint.

Looking back on that hat-buying period in my life, it's clear that it was connected with my changing sense of myself as a man. It's no coincidence that I bought that first one at a time when I was approaching maturity. Like many young men, I mistakenly associated masculinity with my genitalia and the hat provided me with a boost to the security I truly did not feel with the mere possession of a cock and balls. Once adjusted to adult life, however, I was able to rely on my sexual identity to empower my sense of manhood not only, first, as libertine and man-about-town romantic, but eventually as a husband, paterfamilias, breadwinner, and solver of all of life's problems.

By the time I reached my fiftieth year, however, the façade I had built began to show the cracks. Call it mid-life crisis, which I suppose describes it well enough. Having slipped by with nothing but good fortune from school teaching to academia and after devoting years to a professional life in which I never felt comfortable, I finally remembered that I was supposed to be a writer. I knew as much, as my mother reminded me when I was twelve years old because I told her so.

(Don't worry, I'll get back to those hats).

So much for the breadwinner, then. I quit my job and went overnight from earning a comfortable income as an academic dean to scraping a few dollars together as a freelance writer. I was fortunate—and am forever grateful—that Ellie was able to step up to fill the gap, even though there was a good deal of masculine pride I had to learn to swallow. By now successful in her work as an art consultant, she became our primary source of income. By the time I reached my mid-fifties, then, all my assumptions about who as I was a man were thrown into question. Then my father died. My mother died. The family for which I had always taken responsibility spiraled down into a medical, emotional, and psychological crisis. I was confronted with the frightening understanding that I no longer had the answers to everybody's problems—my own included.

Things fell apart, and it took some work to begin to bring them back together. I had to learn, for example, a hard lesson for many men: that the heart is a more consequential organ than the genitals. I had to adjust to life without a job. I still worked, of course. I never stopped working, every day of my life. But no matter how hard I worked I could never generate anything like a salary. I tried writing novels, deluding myself for a brief period into the belief that this would lead to wealth and fame. I even sold a couple of books to reputable publishers. Even so, I had to learn to accept the hard truth that the work of writing is not necessarily paid work, and still to think of it as work. I discovered to my surprise that I still had a lot of growing up to do, along with a good deal of acknowledging past mistakes, atoning for some unskillful actions of the past, and accepting what-is, in the present. I found that to be no small task.

So anyway, about those hats. They were easy enough to change, unlike those hard changes in my life. Their variety made it possible to match them to account for a shift in mood, in temperament. Oddly, they offered me not only an element of disguise but also a sense of security, a sense of identity as the "new man" I was working hard to be. They were playful, too, and fun, a needed diversion from the painful realities of more serious change. I could put a hat on my head and venture out into the world with at least the illusion of confidence.

I don't need hats anymore. I am older, perhaps even wiser. My hair is shorter, as I said, and no longer needs containment. I welcome the sensation of the wind in my hair, a token of freedom in itself. My hats still hang in neat rows on the rack I purchased for them at a swap meet long ago. They remind me of the time I needed them and enjoyed their company, the time they helped me create a new identity or, more properly, new identities. I hold them close today as the best of old friends, loath to say goodbye and still grateful for their reassuring company. But wear them? No. I don't need that anymore.

Grief

I am a fan of Margaret Renkl's columns in the New York Times. Hers is an authentic voice from the American South, and she writes with clarity and compassion about the experience of being human and the pleasure and pain she derives from observing the world around her. She delights in surprising us with what we can learn from our pets and the birds and squirrels in our backyard, as much as from our fellow beings and their foibles.

Her column yesterday was about the nature of grief, in particular the grief that continues to consume her personally long after her parents' death. I read it with a kind of envy for the depth with which she is able to experience and write about her emotions and wondered, as I read, about the immeasurable distance between her ability to experience and express them and my own; whether there is, for example, a real, demonstrable, inborn difference between men and women when it comes to the life of the emotions, or whether it is simply the conventional view that men are brought up in a different way and trained from boyhood on to hide, suppress or deny their feelings for fear of the vulnerability of appearing weak or feminine.

I found myself thinking, as I read, about those I have lost in my own immediate family—my mother and father, my in-laws, and my sister. I search in my heart in vain for feelings as deep as those expressed in the profoundly moving essay I was reading. I wondered whether that might also be because I spent so much of my life away from my family from childhood on and, especially in my parents' later years, the vast geographical distance that lay between us; or whether, sadly, I never simply felt love as intense and intensely personal as Renkl's, and for this reason experienced grief less profoundly than she did. I wondered, too, if there was something lacking in my own humanity, that I was unable to grieve so long and deeply.

I will say this: I grieve more deeply for my sister, who has now already preceded me in death by some eight years. A year and a half older than I, she would have celebrated her eighty-eighth birthday this past February. She died at eighty. Separated as siblings at an early age by being sent off to different boarding schools and then in most of our adult lives by different marriages, different divorces, and finally by an ocean and a continent, it was only late in our lives that our paths began to converge in a common concern with the heart and the life of the mind. I learned much from her in those last years, and her *green* burial beneath a lovely tree on a green English hillside was for me a heart-wrenching experience. I had written a poem for her, *Bluebells*, about picking flowers as children for our mother, and I choked up dreadfully as I read it. I have mourned her loss ever since.

For all these thoughts I am grateful to a writer who can easily access places in the heart that are hard for me to reach, and for showing me the way.

Rhymes

I wake in the middle of the night—at one twenty-six a.m., to be precise—to the realization that my mind has been hard at work making pointless lists of words that rhyme. Try, fry, pry, buy, cry, my, chai... it goes on and on. I try asking it politely to please stop, I want to go back to sleep, but it seems my mind has a mind of its own. It just keeps rhyming. I must have dropped off eventually anyway because I wake again a couple of hours later and find it still at work, having added a consonant this time for variety: right, bright, smite, might, fight, fright, light, polite, incite, contrite... But my mind is not a bit contrite, it insists on churning out these rhymes. What am I going to do with them all? When it runs out of one consonant it starts on another, playing a joke on itself with "rhyme", then time, chime, lime, brine, thine, pine, mine... It seems there's no end of "i" rhymes in the lexicon. Yes, even "mind"—and off I go into mind, bind, find, kind, wind, blind, behind...

And then of course I realize that it's not my mind at all. It's my stupid brain. My mind is bigger, smarter, wiser, and infinitely more powerful than the bundle of 1336 grams of grey matter I keep under my skull. I have been blaming the wrong culprit, begging for merciful relief from the wrong perpetrator. It's only when I summon the power of my mind to come to my assistance that I can um... find... relief. To activate the mind, I know enough to bring another tool to bear: the breath, using it to open the mind to its vast serenity. Then everything drops away, even the rhymes, as the infinite mind-space unveils itself in all its majestic dis-association, inviting me to return to my favorite occupation, resting in radiant awareness. Which is as a good place to be as any I can imagine.

Posing Naked

I was interested to read an article by Rachel Sherman in the Arts section of yesterday's *New York Times* because it brought vividly to mind an experience of my own, many years ago. The article was provocatively titled *I Was a Nude Model for a Half Hour. Revelatory? Actually, Yes!* In it, she reviewed two exhibitions in New York, one of them titled *Yves Klein and the Tangible World* and the other, also provocatively *Get Nude, Get Drawn*.

Both exhibits challenged the vulnerability of the human body. The Yves Klein exhibit featured a white box with a single hole in one side, through which the visitor was invited to reach in and touch the nude figure of its occupant—a live model apparently accustomed to being nude, if less so being touched. Sherman described an almost electrical jolt through the initial contact, followed by moments of surprising—even *touching!*—intimacy as she felt and probed the contour of the body within, arriving at a whole new experience of what it means to be herself living in a naked human body.

I have a surprisingly personal relationship with Yves Klein, who died many years ago at the age of 34. My in-laws, Ellie's parents, were among the small number of collectors buying one of his *Immaterials*, tossing gold ingots at his instruction into the Seine from the Pont Neuf, leaving no trace of the "artwork". (Klein cheated a bit on the *immaterial* part: he had a photographer standing by—without their knowledge—to record the event).

More personal to me, though, was *Get Nude, Get Drawn*, and the memory it conjured of having myself posed naked for the distinguished portrait artist Don Bachardy. He had invited me first to sit fully clothed for one of his familiar portraits, head, shoulders, and torso, and I found the experience so intense, so strangely intimate and objective all at once, that I asked him if I could come back to sit naked. He readily agreed, and I showed up two weeks later and took off all my clothes, allowing him to pose me as he wanted.

I had a good reason for requesting something that I instinctively dreaded, having learned that to confront my fears directly is always to come out ahead of them. It has long been a personal phobia for me, to be seen naked, and the opportunity offered me the chance to face that fear by exposing my body to no mere passing glimpse, but to the intense, unsparing, prolonged scrutiny Bachardy brings to a session in his studio.

It turned out to be an almost exhilarating experience, half-lying there like some less than appealing masculine Venus under Bachardy's steady gaze. He went to work without the slightest suggestion of commentary or judgment. He looked, he saw, he painted what he saw. The connection between us was that between the artist and his model, professional—but no, I'd prefer to avoid that word because I have never much liked it, in that it sounds somehow cold and heartless. It could not be described as a disinterested gaze either, though it had the quality or pure observation. But the interest was earnest, I would almost say loving in its intensity—though with a love for the task at hand rather than for the particular person lying naked on the bed.

Thinking of that white box at the Yves Klein exhibit and the probing nature of that stranger's physical touch, I had something of the experience Sherman describes—not an electric jolt, perhaps, but a comparable sensation of exposure and safety all at once, the gift of one person's most intimate humanity to another—but without the sex!

I will not readily forget that session with Bachardy. It did not entirely "cure" me of that instinctive fear, but it left me more tolerant of my body and its deficiencies and flaws. And despite my critical appraisal, more inclined to concede its very human beauty.

Who We Are

This is the new mantra, a disclaimer that I hear with distressing frequency on the lips of many of our leaders during these dark days: "This is not who we are", they say, often along with its corollary, "We are better than this."

But suppose this *is* who we are? We Americans? Not too long ago our country elected a man to lead us whom we knew to be petty, vindictive, undisciplined, mercenary, self-interested, wholly lacking in compassion, and quick to blame anyone other than himself for his every weakness, failure, and transgression. His term in office was marked by incompetence—deadly, in his handling of the Covid crisis—favoritism, nepotism, and corruption. He denied election results and fought to stay in power after voters evicted him from office, urging supporters to storm the Capitol. Incredibly, as of this writing, one-half of America is poised to elect him again, even though he stands indicted on 91 felony counts—and already convicted on 34. Abusing a justice system he has manipulated into compliance, he has succeeded in delaying trials on every other charge until after the next election. Meanwhile, he has co-opted the entire Republican Party whose leaders kowtow to him, cringingly unable to speak the truth and promising to vote for his re-election, all the while acknowledging his unfitness for office behind his back. Even those of us who harshly opposed him are now endlessly subject to his whims, held firmly in his thrall by the media attention he demands and the political power he wields.

I say *we*, meaning we Americans, much though I'd like to dissociate myself from this shambolic situation because *we* must hold ourselves accountable for allowing such a man to dominate our lives. Is *he* what we deserve? Does *he* reflect our values? Alas, far from not being "who we are," he is the mirror image in which others see us and, if we are honest, we ought to see ourselves. It is past time for us to examine these difficult truths about ourselves. We should be looking into our own hearts and souls for what is petty, vindictive, undisciplined, mercenary, self-interested, lacking in compassion, and quick to blame others for our faults. We must stop comforting ourselves with the bromide that "this is not who we are" and instead engage in some serious soul-searching and be prepared to make changes where we find them necessary.

These thoughts have been simmering in the back of my mind for some time and have begun to bubble uncomfortably to the surface every time I hear those exculpatory words. Even our current President utters them, and he is plainly a good and decent man. I thought of them again recently as I watched the final episodes of *The Staircase*, a television documentary in which a man is pursued—persecuted is not too strong a word—by a court system unconcerned with discovering the truth and dispensing justice but rather using all its resources to win the case against this one scapegoat and exact vengeance. This shameless attack includes invented or distorted evidence, junk science, outright perjury, and every conceivable form of judicial chicanery. After fifteen years of institutional abuse—and eight of those years in prison—the target of this pernicious "investigation" attains his freedom and a grudging measure of justice, but only in exchange for a specious guilty plea that is demanded of him even as he persists in his unwavering claims of innocence.

Is this who we are; a judicial system in which police and prosecutors, locked into the righteousness of an a priori assumption of a person's guilt, are willing to do whatever it takes to prove their case? Are we the people who sit idly by and watch as our fellow men and women are convicted of serious crime based on false evidence and junk science, and serve long prison sentences before being exonerated by a simple DNA test? Appallingly, men are put to death despite convincing evidence of their innocence.

Are we that people?

In the same vein, we empower our police to administer "justice" on the streets, without the benefit of arrest or trial. To simply be black or brown is to be suspect, arrested, sometimes to die at the hands of law enforcement. How can we continue to pretend that "this is not who we are" when we are willing to condemn the innocent while the rich and the powerful go free, those able to buy the justice they do not deserve? When one of our political parties seeks to violate the entire justice system to exculpate a man found guilty by a jury of his peers, based only on their subservience to his whims?

Who are we really? According to multiple polls and surveys we claim to be a religious people, but the reality we create makes a mockery of every known religion. In social programs enacted in our name, we show little care for the sick, the poor, and the hungry. Quite the opposite. In its obsession with "big government spending," our representative majority is intent on shredding an already tenuous social safety net; reversing the minimal health insurance plan that was so narrowly and grudgingly approved; eviscerating the public education system while providing the generous tax breaks to the rich that allow them to benefit from private education. And that's not to mention our propensity for violence, with increasing numbers of states passing legislation to allow us to tote weapons of war on our public streets while the number of mass shootings and domestic violence deaths continues to climb. We lay claim to "family values" with sentimental ardor, yet we fail to protect our own families when they encounter difficulties, let alone those who seek refuge at our borders. Yes, true, I am a bleeding-heart liberal—what we used to call a socialist before the word was sullied in the American lexicon—but you and I, my citizen friend, cannot ingenuously disclaim responsibility for such things. They reflect who we are.

No matter how we profess belief in democratic values and the principle of universal suffrage, many of those in power are now resorting to every trick to restrict access to the polls. Claiming powerlessness as individuals, we risk the surrender of our vaunted democracy to the wealthiest of our fellow citizens. The truth about us, if we care to admit it, is that we have watched the decades-long creation of an oligarchy controlled by corporate interests and billionaires who can determine the outcome of elections with unaccountable campaign contributions and deploy their lobbying power to create laws that favor their interests. In the past we made pious claims to be the model of democracy in the community of nations, but now many in power grovel at the feet of tyrants and dictators and parrot their propaganda.

Finally, not least, we embrace the public display of ostentatious, contentious America First patriotism, requiring our politicians to wrap themselves piously in the flag. We profess a profound love of our country, with all the wonders of its natural beauty and rich resources even as the government we elect allows its degradation by those whose only interest is in financial gain. We create the lion's share of global pollution, even as we surrender to those who dismiss the evidence of competent science. We make a great show of wringing our hands but fail to act as the leaders we should be.

I acknowledge that I write these thoughts from a place of privilege—an enviable education, social status, and relative financial security. And enough with the jeremiad. It's true that there is much that is good about us, witness our quick response to tragedy or catastrophe, neighbor eager to help neighbor, forgetting differences in those moments when we come together in a common cause. We share, when occasion arises, a spirit of generosity, kindness, compassion. This is the truth invoked by those who insist that "we are better than this."

If so, it's time for us to stop casting blame on others and take responsibility for the actions taken, or neglected, in our name. It's time to take a long, unsparing look at who we risk becoming, and set about the work that's needed to become the "we" we would like to believe ourselves to be—work that requires the sacrifice of petty interests and promotes mutual understanding, tolerance and compromise. And if we really want to retain and refresh our democracy, it's work that requires our vote, our friends' votes, and the votes of the friends of our friends.

But we can do this, surely? Because isn't this "who we are?"

The Boss

I tell you, sometimes I think I could throttle this *writer* fellow who occupies my inner space and claims my life. Or at least get him to shut up. Retire, perhaps. Trouble is, he's a persistent *cuss*, and something of an insomniac. He wakes me up at four, four-thirty, five in the morning, eager to get started, and won't allow me to get back to sleep. He has an annoyingly imperious streak, insisting that I act as his humble scribe, taking down dictation, making notes, issuing peremptory orders and reminders. With a boss like this, who needs a real one?

As I say, I could sometimes throttle him.

Ten of Us

There are ten of us now. The youngest is 70. At 87, I am the oldest. Some of us are still involved in the men's training weekends offered by The ManKind Project, the organization that brought us together in the first place, and still brings us together now, in a group that we dedicate to what we call "conscious aging." All of us have led or served on staff at those weekends, some of us many times. We have all learned the critical importance of "the work" in our lives—the work of tireless self-examination, of truthfulness, of clear intention. Over many years now, this work has provided tens of thousands of men worldwide with the opportunity to examine their lives, acknowledge what works and what doesn't, and to come away with a renewed sense of purpose, a new dedication to authenticity and integrity, a new mission of service to their fellow human beings. For most of the past six thousand years, we men have taken ourselves for granted as the dominant force in Western culture, but to cast a glance around the world today is to recognize that despite all our considerable steps of progress from the caves, we have fallen short in many ways. If the world—the Earth itself—is to survive its current crisis, we need to find masculine leaders who are less damaged by unacknowledged wounds, less shaped by what is wrongly considered the archetype of male strength and authority.

So here we are, all ten of us. We are geographically far apart. Our meeting is made possible by Zoom, where we each fit into our own little box on the computer screen. The ideal would be to meet in person, of course, but we have a core connection that makes this virtual meeting acceptable. It lifts my spirits to see these faces, hear these voices, to know that this is a space where I will be heard, honored, trusted, no matter what; and where I can listen to voices whose authenticity I accept without question. What a blessing and a joy to have this safe haven. Even though we meet for one hour only, and only twice a month, it pleases me to know this place is here for me. It pleases me, too, to know that I have earned my place, as each of the others has earned his, through many years of work and dedication to the cause we all acknowledge without having to speak its name. If pressed to do so, we might call it healing.

Our topic for discussion this evening is... women! I raise the subject in the context of a book authored by another long-time member of our organization. In his book, I have followed him page by page through his troubled early years and, finally, his commitment to a woman he has come to love with an intensity that is almost unbearable, through the birth of their two sons; and up to the moment where their marriage begins to fall apart. There is what he calls a "dissolution," despite what he believes to be his earnest efforts to hold things together. I raise the issue out of concern for a young woman close to me, a single mom, who is presently confused about where she is in her life. Feeling less than comfortable in her job, she is struggling to maintain a loving but long-distance relationship... and wants more out of love and life. She loves the man, and he undoubtedly loves her, but she's looking for consistent, day-to-day companionship, a helpmate in the demanding life she has created for herself.

As usual, as has always been the case, the first thing on my mind is how to "help". How to fix the problem. Sitting in our virtual circle I hear the support of other men—men who, like me, have lived for many years thinking they are duty-bound to fix things, especially for the women in their lives. However patronizing, it comes with the conventional territory of being a man among women and the unquestioning assumption that we know better, that we have the answers. This, even when we often manage to make a mess of our own lives! We flatter ourselves to be God's gift to our helpless mates. One member of our group, a man who is now on his fourth marriage after three failures, speaks up to tell us how he finally learned a long overdue lesson from his latest wife. He had been listening—he thought patiently—to her woes and was all ready to set her straight with some basic truths when she held up her hand to stop him. What she needed, she said, was not to have her anxiety explained away; she just needed him to listen. After all those years of marriage, and failed marriages, it finally came to him as a revelation: all that was needed of him was to listen. Since then, he has learned to catch himself before automatically reaching for the answer, rather than asking the simple question: "How can I support you?"

I know this. I should know it. I learned long ago that my attempts to fix things were unwelcome and unasked for. But it was good to be reminded. To judge by other feedback in the group, each one of us was grateful to be reminded of what we all learned long ago, and what is easy to forget. We don't have all the answers. We slip unconsciously into the old, learned fix-it mode. Before we realize it, we find ourselves speaking with the voice of male authority and being offended if we are not heard. Or to be honest, not obeyed. I am myself an inveterate backslider, skillfully passing over everything I have learned and becoming, once again, the One Who Knows.

I have good reason, then, to feel gratitude, having men of such integrity who will not hesitate to remind me when I risk losing mine. They speak with respect for my advancing years and my failing memory, but with uncompromising clarity and insight. Like most men, I find it hard to say out loud that I love another man, but with these friends, I can say truthfully that these are men I love.

Witness

It was a simple conflict, one that would seem to be easily resolved. So why, I asked myself, did my mind insist on making such a big deal of it—big enough to wake me up at an ungodly hour this morning and refuse to let me go back to sleep?

It may seem trivial, but bear with me. The conflict was on its face a matter of scheduling, a clash between two events taking place at the same time. The first was the monthly meeting with my conscious aging group. I have known most of these men for years and have worked with them on problems great and small, from transient trivialities all the way up to the meaning and purpose of our lives. These are men I love and trust, and men whose trust I have earned. Not something to be taken lightly. The second event was purely political and might seem of little importance by comparison. It was a televised congressional committee meeting addressing an issue that seemed to me critical for the well-being of this country I have chosen to make my home. My social conscience tells me it's important to pay attention to such things. So which one should take preference?

There was a catch: I knew quite well that advances in technology would allow me to record the televised hearing and start watching it an hour later—something I would obviously be unable to do with our men's meeting on Zoom. In the latter, too, I am personally involved in the interaction that takes place between us. My showing up is important not only to myself but to my friends. No one other than myself would know or care if I tuned in late to an event taking place in my absence, and without my participation, on the stage of national affairs. My presence in front of a television screen would make no difference to any living person—or indeed to the proceedings.

Pure logic would seem to make the choice an easy one. And yet it wasn't. I was torn, in a way I could not have anticipated. I told myself that this was ridiculous, that I was making far too much of a very small thing, but in the middle of the night that argument remained unpersuasive to my busy mind, which persisted in pursuing the debate surrounding this seemingly specious dilemma. The conflict *felt* like a challenge to my integrity, about doing the right thing.

So why? Why the attachment to an event that I could watch only remotely, through the television set, unable to actively participate and with absolutely no control? I think because I sensed its critical importance to the preservation of this peculiarly American experiment in democracy that has survived, despite all obstacles and adversities, this past quarter of a millennium. The outcome of this session would affect not only the direction of my adoptive country but potentially also the survival of the human species and the planet we are given to inhabit. Humanity itself is at a turning point, and this moment had become its focus. I felt an inner urgency to be *present* for it in the best way possible, not as a bystander to history seeking "news" or "information," but as one called on to bear witness. I felt the need to be present for the debate, participating in a ritual upon which the fate of humanity might depend.

The debate rages on, despite my other need—for sleep! I lie there, castigating myself for making too much of a decision that matters not a whit to anyone other than myself. It irks me, as I watch my mind in turmoil, not to be able to simply switch it off like any other device. Am I losing it?

Is it any wonder that I've been losing sleep?

Uncouth

As one who has felt obligated from his earliest days to be unfailingly, blamelessly, and even sometimes pointlessly polite, I often stop to wonder how I managed to end up in a country where so many of my fellow citizens seem, er... uncouth.

There's a word! Uncouth. Its etymology may be cloudy, but its meaning is pleasingly precise: in my personal lexicon, it means rude, disrespectful, brash, and uncivilized.

Is it uncouth to mention this?

I look around me and am distressed to see so much churlish behavior. Civility—deference when appropriate, respect, and common decency—seems like a lost cause, not only in personal relationships but in society at large, not to mention in the political arena where the idea of service is replaced by a cutthroat lust for power.

The fine Buddhist principles of Right Speech and Right Action (words I try to live by, from the Noble Eightfold Path) are notably absent from much of our public discourse and interaction.

Even what were once reliable principles of politeness have fallen into disuse. I was brought up, for example, to respect that quaint injunction: Ladies First! These days, if I care to affirm a woman's rights and honor her hard-won independence, should I open the door and step through ahead of her, or should I stand back, as I was taught to do, and hold the door open—and risk insulting her? Holding the door is a habit so deeply ingrained that I am physically incapable of passing ahead of anyone, man, woman, child. I stand there like an idiotic, overly zealous doorman until the last person in line has gone through.

To be sure, this is a trivial example but as see it, such acts of simple civility are a grievous loss in our contemporary world. In what universe, not long ago, would it have been considered acceptable to sit in a restaurant staring intently at the little screen on your telephone while everyone around you does the same? Or loudly conduct your personal business while others try to eat? Worse, in what world would it be thought civil to intrude on your private telephone to sell you something you don't want or need? Since when did it become acceptable to receive a gift or enjoy dinner at a friend's without a word of thanks?   For that matter, since when was it normal to drive on city streets as though no other vehicles existed?

Small things, yes. But they offend every instinct that was hammered into me as a child. I'm sure that the thoughts of the stuffy old British gentlemen that I foolishly remain heart will seem quaint to readers these days, but I persist in wondering grumpily how the human species will survive without the kind of behavior that's guided by a sense of mutual respect.

Bumpkin

I have been challenged to take another look at myself in light of recent online exchanges with a fellow writer who often responds to my social media posts. His comments are always welcome. He is smart, well-informed, a well-known and nationally published art critic. He is also an accomplished and dedicated painter and remains an unapologetic intellectual—and no disrespect for that! The word "urbane" comes to mind. An exacting rationalist, he takes pleasure in poking holes in my every lapse in logic—of which there are admittedly many. He is also an uncompromising atheist in the manner of Daniel Dennett, Richard Dawkins, Christopher Hitchens, and others, dismissing any suggestion of religious or spiritual belief as *woo-woo*.

Always grateful to someone who challenges my assumptions and makes me think again, I see myself and this friend (I first missed that "r" and wrote "fiend!") at opposite poles. I too was for many years a widely published writer about art and artists, but never so rigorous or knowledgeable as he, and the outlets for my reviews and articles are no match for his. I do not share his intellectual rigor.

I have come to realize that I remain a country bumpkin at heart. For many years I managed to play the part of an intellectual, and quite successfully so. But I never felt comfortable in that role. Though I climbed the educational ladder to the dizzying heights of a doctorate and spent a good number of years as a teacher in the academic world, I was finally forced to recognize that I never belonged there in the first place. I quit that world a long time ago now and have been much happier since.

It took me many years, however, to arrive at the understanding that the little boy brought up in an English country village lives on at my innermost core. It's just who I am. Polite, if sometimes mischievous. A bit simple-minded, perhaps. A lover of nature, more so than of books, music, or art. Tending to accept what is for what it is. Less at home in the big city than in a village or a little seaside town. Easily awed and lacking, for the most part, in guile or ill-will. Kind of innocent, I guess. Wide-eyed. No longer a believer in the God I was brought up with but certainly in things greater than myself, things invested in meaning that transcends the merely explicable or utile. And willing to blurt out whatever happens to be on my mind at any given moment.

There's a John Denver song whose chorus goes *Thank God I'm a country boy!* That's me. But an English country boy, not an American one. There's a difference. The one is rough and ready, the other reticent, a bit naïve, a bit credulous. A bit like me.

Purple Ice Cream

It was an unusually cold night, 42 degrees Fahrenheit, or "freezing" as we call it here in Southern California. I woke very early, 4:15 AM. Climbed out of bed to switch on the heat and staggered off to answer nature's call, and when I got back to bed, I couldn't sleep. Couldn't sleep and couldn't sleep, worried about nothing more serious than the clutter in our house. But I must have eventually dropped off because I woke from a dream...

Ellie and Luka and I were invited to join a big clean-up party outside the front of a very rich gay man's mansion (I know who it is, but I'm not telling here; he's not nearly so rich as he was in the dream, and he doesn't live in a mansion...) It's dirty work, involving digging up drains to fix the plumbing so far as I can tell, and there's a lunch break with a big spread set out at formal tables. I must be a late arrival because all that's left to eat is a few thick slices of bread, and inexplicably the chef will only allow me half a slice and a single lettuce leaf.

We tuck in. The wealthy man sits at the head table with a row of beautiful young men on either side of him. He seems to have selected one of them for his attention, turning on all his charm as he addresses a ginger-haired lad with freckles and a shy demeanor, who seems to be hard of hearing. After lunch, the two of them go off into the mansion for a post-prandial siesta, and I note to Ellie that we have just observed an object lesson in the art of seduction.

There is a separate station for dessert and Luka and I head off in that direction. There is quite a crowd gathered at the serving table. They are offering a pale green pistachio ice cream that appeals to me, and I request a bowl from the serving woman—another ginger-haired individual; what is it with me and ginger hair, I wonder? She grudgingly serves up a hard, frozen slice of something quite different, a purple ice cream, which is not what I'd ordered. I hope that Luka fares better.

We return to our workstations after dessert, but I realize that before getting back to the job at hand I need to visit the bathroom. Luka goes with me, and we follow a long path alongside the great mansion's façade but fail to find an entrance. Heading back, we discover that the path has now disappeared and that we need to make our way through thick brambles and up sudden, steep slopes of brickwork, clinging to branches where we can find them to avoid slipping in the mud.

After much trouble, we find ourselves in what appears to be the workshop of a palatial art school, an immensely high pavilion with dozens, hundreds of carpentry tools dangling down on wires from the glass ceiling. A student approaches and passes by without a word. We return to our workstation, still not yet having found a bathroom, and I realize that we will certainly need to find one. We are both head-to-toe filthy with mud and grime, and badly need to wash up before going back to work...

Doctor, Doctor

This morning, I am scheduled for a telephone appointment with my doctor. She is concerned—as am I—about the low-grade depression I have been experiencing recently. She has suggested prescribing a medication to help raise my spirits.

I have been wondering how best to describe the feeling of gloom that frequently overwhelms me these days. Some of the words that come to mind are powerlessness, uselessness, and irrelevance. I feel it in my body, a physical sensation. I am still strong, but do not actually *feel* that strength. Walking, I feel no spring in my step; I tend to shuffle around like the old man that I truly am, no denying it. When I follow the exercise routine I learned from the physical therapist I've worked with, they have begun to feel more like a chore than something I look forward to. I try to do them regularly, but life often intervenes. It pains me no end that a combination of age and prostate medications deprives me of the ability to perform sexually, an intensely intimate human function that has previously always brought joy into my life.

When it comes to my personal and professional life, I have been feeling the same kind of powerlessness. I am an accomplished writer; that is my strength. Yet the use of my skills is no longer accompanied by the same sense of pleasure and power. I look back on everything I have written and can bask in a certain sense of success. I have published widely over a long period now—books, magazine and newspaper articles, and critical reviews. I have posted in a series of successful and widely read blogs. I continue to maintain a presence on social media, and I know that my writing brings pleasure to those who read what I post. From time to time I hear that something I have written has changed someone's life—news that never fails to bring me joy. Today, though, when I sit down to write I have no sense of urgency.

I have always considered it my responsibility as a man to make a difference in the world, a contribution, yet now the feeling is irrelevance. A part of it is the big picture. I inherited from my father a strong social conscience; I feel the need to be doing something useful. I look around today, late in my life, and see little but pain and chaos in the world, especially here in America, the country in which I arrived more than 60 years ago with boundless hope. I see callousness and cruelty, greed and selfishness, hunger for power, and unconcern for the suffering of others. Seeing all this, I feel that same powerlessness, that same irrelevance, and it pains me. I feel guilty for not having the motivation to do more.

But then I look back at the weekend just past and am amazed at how the depression lifted for a time. I felt lighter and stronger. Our son Jason was visiting from Iowa; our daughter Sarah was here, with her twelve-year-old son, Luka. Ellie was delighting in her role as mother and grandmother. What conquered the depression, I realize as I look back, was love—the love I was able to give and the love that I received. I felt needed, respected, and empowered by the presence of family. I could bask in my own effortless, unproblematic role as paterfamilias.

I will share some of this with my doctor. More important, though, is the realization that to address the depression myself, without artificial stimulants, I need only to love more, and better, and learn to love myself as well as others. That, as the saying goes, is the ticket.

Headache

I woke last night in the middle of the night from a dream that I had a dreadful headache and soon realized that I did in fact have a dreadful headache. I lay there in bed wondering whether the dream had started the headache, or the headache had prompted the dream. Kind of chicken and egg. And then quite suddenly I realized that I did not actually have a headache at all.

Funny thing, the mind. It does love to play its tricks.

Wasps

A couple of days ago our daughter Sarah, down for the weekend with our grandson Luka, drew my attention to a buzzing sound from behind one of the pictures on the wall in our living room. I took the picture down and found a wasp-like creature behind, buzzing away. I took the whole picture to the front door and let the insect fly out, free. Put the picture back. Feeling good. An act of compassionate liberation. Good Buddhist practice.

A wasp, Ellie thought. I thought differently. The insect was too elongated for a wasp, I pointed out, its front and back ends separated by a long-ish narrow thread. Not a wasp. I wondered if it had a sting…

Well and good. An incident easily forgotten. The next morning, though, I thought to hear the same buzzing sound coming from behind the same picture (a small, atypical color drawing by James Hayward, for those interested, bi-chrome, two goldish monochrome sections parted just above the middle by a hazy horizon line. Very nice, but irrelevant to my story). I took the picture down again and another wasp flew out into the living room and buzzed off. This time, though, I noticed something I had missed before, a smallish gray lump attached to the paper that backed the picture frame. A nest, I wondered? Could these creatures be hatching from that strange lump?

Curious now, I turned to the ever-helpful Google. It appears there are many kinds of wasps. Who knew? Well, an entomologist, I suppose. But not me. I searched through the images and decided that our visitors were... mud dauber wasps! They sting, but "only when they are threatened', as Luka told me, having done his own research on Google. (I had by now started an online conversation with my grandson about this whole adventure. "Cool", he wrote.)

Our tentative identification was confirmed when I decided that behind the James Hayward was not the optimal place for a wasp's nest-- not even if it was a mud dauber wasp. I took the picture out to the balcony and scraped off what was clearly... hardened mud! Poking at the resulting debris I saw a bunch of tiny brown spots which on closer examination proved to be an earlier stage of the hatchlings that had come crawling out. Mud dauber wasp babies! Obviously, tiny as they were, they had no chance of survival outside their womb. Not knowing what else to do, I found a brush and swept them down between the cracks of the deck. I felt terrible of course. Even a not-quite Buddhist like myself is upset by the thought of killing any living being. But what else was I to do?

You might think that was the end of the story. No. I was not to be spared even further guilt. A short time later, and quite often after that. we noticed a mud dauber wasp hovering near the picture, quite clearly in a repeated search of what was once the nest. A mother mud dauber wasp, I thought! It had to be. Looking for her babies!

Well, you can imagine how I felt, a confirmed mass murderer now, who had cruelly deprived a mother of her offspring. What a monster! I sat this morning in meditation and tried to restore a little karmic credit for my callous act. I don't know if I succeeded, and I guess I never will—unless I am to be born again in some appropriately monstrous form!

A Letter

Dear Friend,

Something you said a few days ago has been on my mind, and I've been mulling it over. What you wrote—I hope I have this right—is that you've tried meditation and have discovered that it just doesn't work for you. I hear something similar from many smart, thoughtful people like yourself, for whom I have great admiration. They know that I sit every day, but likely don't know that I told myself the same thing for a good number of years before I embarked on my 25-year practice: that my mind was just too busy.

I don't want to proselytize, but when good people tell me that meditation is great for other people but not for them, I'm inclined to think they believe that in meditation the mind must become a purely passive organ where all thought is switched off at will and becomes a kind of placid non-entity, a dreaded vacuum.

For me, though, meditation is not like that at all. It's not even especially hard—that is, if I remember not to keep telling myself how hard it is. Or especially, how boring! It's in fact quite pleasant to sit quietly for a while and watch with interest as the breath does what it's supposed to do, entering and exiting the body, leaving it refreshed and fully oxygenated. If thoughts come along, as they will, it's not so hard to watch with polite interest—and without getting attached—as they do their peculiar, always fascinating dance. It's kind of entertaining. And watching the mind go to work is not incompatible with meditation. On the contrary, it's the whole point: all the better to be in charge and able to put it to good use.

Is meditation a "spiritual" exercise? This is another stumbling block for many—as it was, for years, for me. Some practice it as such. I know that you disparage anything that has to do with what that inadequate word implies, and for well-founded intellectual reasons—reasons I respect and tend to share. I am agnostic in these matters: I emphatically do not believe in God, but nor am I willing to totally dismiss the thought and practice that have distinguished religions for centuries of human history. There is much of value, I believe, much to learn. And I believe there is a certain arrogance in those who dismiss it with such certainty.

But this is not why I meditate. I meditate for one purely practical reason: to take care of the mind. To provide it, so to speak, with the nutrition, the exercise and yes, the rest that it needs, just as the body does. The mind is the most powerful tool we have—by multitudes of ratios more powerful than the brain. Those of us who are fortunate enough to enjoy the privileges of status, material well-being, relative financial security, and family security typically spend a great deal of time, energy, and money taking care of our bodies with a healthy diet, exercise, sensible medical attention, rest, and so on. Why not take equal care of the mind?

The value of the practice, as I see it, is to train the mind to do those things I ask of it, rather than allow it to run wild with anything that crosses its path. I see it primarily as a discipline, a training. It's not for nothing that seasoned meditators use the metaphor of the puppy dog needing to be trained. Focus and concentration are the immediate benefits. The bigger, long-term, and more elusive goal is happiness and peace of mind, or what Buddhists call "the end of suffering." I don't presume to lay claim to great success—Zen mind, beginner's mind, and all that!—but at least I can say that it continues to be worth the effort.

Anyway, forgive me for intruding on your time and patience. I don't mean to preach—and I don't like unsolicited preachers. But what you said provoked these thoughts, and I just wanted to get them "off my mind." It's just talk… And I do enjoy our occasional verbal jousts.

Sending the best of wishes from your friend,

Peter

Letting Go

Everyone has something they need to let go. The Buddha, in his wisdom, taught that attachment is the cause of suffering. We get attached to images of ourselves, to outcomes, to ideas and feelings, to what we imagine we need. So yesterday, in the circle of our artist-friends that meets each month—and after a few minutes of meditation—Ellie was inspired to start the meeting off with the mention of something she needed to let go of. Her thoughts inspired me, in turn. to suggest a round in which we would each use a single word to say what we needed to release. I thought it would be a great way to set the tone for our meeting.

It proved to be, for me at least, an emotional moment. We went around the circle and everyone dug deep and found something, and I think we all recognized ourselves in what others needed to let go. When my turn came—I was last—the word popped up spontaneously: the future. I need to let go of the future.

There is so much that attaches me to the future. I am particularly attached, at this moment, to tidying up the mess I have spent a lifetime accumulating—books, papers, manuscripts, photographs, financial records, and memorabilia of all kinds. None of these things is of possible use or interest to anyone other than me, and even to myself no longer. It's a mess of *stuff* I have determined not to leave for others to clean up.

I'm attached, too, to the completion of this book that I'm just now working to finish. Will I ever get done with it before I die? What will I do with it when I do?

I'm attached to outcomes, then, some of them quite risible: will humans ever get to Mars? Others are deadly serious: will we humans ever succeed in cleaning up the much greater mess we have all made of this planet? Will our grandchildren find the solutions needed to address the pollution that threatens to suffocate our species? Our great-grandchildren? Will they even have a habitable planet to enjoy, with flowers and trees, oceans and animals, as we have done?

I'm attached to whether we will ever get rid of the former President. Even if voters reject him in the next election, will he accept their verdict this time if the vote goes against him? Will we ever be able to erase his giant shadow from our collective consciousness? Or will we be trying to rid ourselves of him off until he dies? Or after? Will his demented vision live on after him in the cult he leaves behind? Will his lies be exposed? Will those who worship him one day find their true religion elsewhere?

I'm even more deeply attached to what we personally will do if he and his Republican enablers win the next election. Like so many people we know, Ellie and I talk of finding some other place to live. But none of our talk is realistic. Where in the world would we go? Our roots here are so entangled and so deep—and we are so old! How could we ever uproot ourselves and find a climate where people like us, spoiled by countless years in temperate Southern California, could survive? No joke, as Uncle Joe Biden would say!

None of these attachments to the future bring me happiness and most of them are not mine to control. It's the familiar wisdom of the serenity prayer to "accept those things I cannot change" and I aspire to that wisdom. Meantime, however, I also need to find "the courage to change the things I can." And I can clean up my own mess, or at least I can make a good start on the job. I need to get to those dozens of boxes in the garage, where decades of writing, published and unpublished, are waiting for the scrap heap.

My prevarication reminds me that it's not easy, letting go.

Spiritual

That word again. I have said often enough that I have difficulty with it. It has been so much trivialized in endless, multiple attempts to describe that aspect of the human experience that defies accurate definition that it has degenerated into easy shorthand for religion *lite*, New Age cliché, mumbo-jumbo, trendy, quasi-religious movements that go in and out of style. It is also variously referred to as soul, animus and anima, consciousness, mind—but none of these words is adequate.

I long ago found a useful map to all this in the ancient belief that there are four corners to the human experience: body, intellect, feelings and yes, for want of a better word, spirit. When these four are in balance, or "integrated," I think of this as the quality of integrity.

Spirit represents everything in its corner that transcends the other three. The quality of courage, for example, may comprise the physical body; it may also comprise thought and feeling. But there is an element to courage that can't be reduced to any one of the other three, nor to a combination of them. The same applies, as I see it, to the impulse to create a work of art; it involves intellect, the physical body and the feelings it seeks both to express and evoke in response. But the combination of these three is not sufficient to explain it. At its best, it is a genuine expression of the human spirit.

The spirit can also reveal itself in numerous other ways. It can manifest as intuition, imagination; as aspiration, ambition, the need to serve others; as altruism, generosity, empathy, concern for other beings. It can appear in the guise of goodness, love, passion, or compassion. We also call it consciousness, or mind, far bigger and more powerful than the brain. It appears in the guise of religious beliefs, myth, mysticism, and ritual. Then, too, the spirit has its dark side, manifesting as vengeance, hatred, and evil. Each of these qualities involves the emotions, certainly, as well as at times the intellect and the physical body, but no one of them, and no combination of them is sufficient to define it.

Some religions teach that spirit is the aspect of mortal humanity that survives after death. But, especially since the dawn of the Age of Reason, many genuinely thoughtful and ethical people scoff at this notion, discounting it as mere sentiment or wishful thinking. Agnostic in this matter myself, I have found no good reason to support belief in an afterlife; but nor can anyone show me convincing evidence that beliefs that have survived centuries of teaching, debate, and sometimes violent antagonisms have no validity worthy of my respect, if not my concurrence.

The dogma of multiple incarnations, for example, remains for me the chief obstacle to a whole-hearted embrace of Buddhism, but I have it on good authority from the most estimable Buddhist source I know that it's fruitless to bother my head about such speculation. So I just go ahead with my meditation practice, which keeps me in daily contact with that part of my humanity that can best be called spirit. Or, for those who have trouble with spirit, then mind. I devote time and effort to taking care of the other aspects of my being—body, intellect, emotions—so why would I not devote equal time and effort to taking care of this aspect of my life? This, for me, is one of the purposes and benefits of daily meditation, and it brings its rewards in the form of peace of mind, stability, and yes, even a measure of that most elusive of qualities, happiness. Not material happiness, nor bodily well-being, nor intellectual gratification. I'm talking about a different kind of happiness, the kind that depends on nothing and no one but the inner self. The kind that is unassailable. The kind that lasts.

The Fox and The Crow

As I've mentioned before, sometimes my feats of memory surprise me. This morning, taking Jake for his early walk, we spotted a big black crow following our every move from his perch on a telephone wire above. Immediately—surprisingly—my mind made a swift trip back to *Le Corbeau et le Renard*, the poem by LaFontaine that I'd had to learn by heart in its French original at the age of eight—or suffer a few sharp raps over the knuckles from Mrs. Smith's wooden ruler. Eighty years ago! I remember it even now, word for word, in its entirety.

The fable is about the crow who holds a tasty piece of cheese in his beak, but is shamelessly flattered by the wily fox below, "*ouvre un large bec, laisse tomber sa proie*"—"opens his beak wide and drops his prey." The fox grabs it with a reminder to the foolish crow (here comes the moral): "*Apprenez que tout flatteur/vit au dépens de celui qui l'écoute*" ("learn that every flatterer lives at the expense of the person who believes him")—and makes off with his plunder.

I was flattered by a reader a while ago for having an excellent memory. "Only for the truly important things," I wrote back. I guess that this was one of them.

On a more serious note, we were talking in my sitting group this past Sunday, Father's Day, after our usual hour of meditation, about fathers, and fatherhood; about our responsibility for our children and how they turn out; and more than a century of psycho-babble and heavy guilt-trips about parents and their kids, and kids and their parents; and finally about the Buddhist teaching about karma, and whether it absolves us from responsibility. One of my fellow-sitters recalled that I was sent off to boarding school at the age of seven and wanted to know what effect it had on my life. And thinking back I remembered my young childhood years, a time of almost idyllic, unalloyed happiness in the village where we lived, when my father was God in my eyes, standing up there at the altar in his church, the glow of multi-colored light from the stained-glass window above him, offering communion, hands raised in blessing for his flock... And the words just tumbled out of my mouth as I finished my story: "...and God sent me away when I was seven years old." And, listening to myself, I realized the enormity of what I'd just said. A small boy, a child, being sent away by the God whom he has been taught for so long to believe is loving.

I have given a great deal of thought to this moment of separation in the many years that have passed since then, but I had never thought of it in quite that way before.

So yes, memories... how some persist inexplicably in our minds and return to the surface of consciousness in sudden, brilliant illumination of epiphanies like this.. And others, as we age—particularly the important ones, the ones we vainly search for when we need them!— slip off maddeningly into oblivion.

Mondrian

I had a wonderful dream last night. I had been having trouble sleeping, waking at 3 AM and unable to get back to sleep. But I must have eventually dropped off into a very deep sleep because I did not wake again until four hours later, nearly 8 o'clock, unusually late for me, and found myself in a state of bliss that must have been brought on by this early morning dream...

I dreamt that I used to visit the late, great artist Piet Mondrian, who was now a gentle, diminutive old man, a Yoda, living in a damp cave downstream from one of those ridiculously expensive resort hotels (was my mind making an association with the ridiculously expensive Mondrian Hotel on Sunset Boulevard?) in a beautiful glen beside a meandering stream. Everything in this grove was a magical, luminescent green—the leaves of the tall trees, the reeds, and grasses by the stream, the moss at the entrance to the Mondrian's cave... Breathtaking!

I was introduced to the great artist by his acolytes, a group of women in the arts led by the legendary Josine Ianco-Starrels (hello, Josine, wherever you are!), a true lover of art and a stalwart friend to artists and people in the art community, including Ellie and myself (I remember that she used to love our daughter Sarah when she was just a little girl...)

I was always welcomed with heart-warming graciousness by the artist on later visits when I went there by myself. His eyes would light up when he saw me, and he would break into a beautiful, warm smile of recognition. He never had much to say, but I felt so honored to be his friend. I used to take him drinks—vodka, I think, was his favorite.

Then Ellie came to stay at the hotel with our grandson, Luka, and I wanted them to experience the same honor that I felt. Before taking them down to the cave, however, I needed a lunchtime sandwich and a glass of vodka, but when I placed my order, I was told that the restaurant closed at 2:30 PM. and it was now a few minutes later. Outraged, I called for the manager, who arrived in black coattails and striped trousers with a neatly tied black tie. He was at first intransigent. The rules were rules. But when I told him I was a friend of Piet Mondrian he underwent a complete transformation. Suddenly friendly, obsequious even, he ordered the staff to bring me whatever I wanted.

After lunch, we walked down alongside the stream, the three of us, Ellie, Luka, and I, and were anticipating the coming meeting with great joy. Sadly, though, the dream came to an end before we reached the cave... I woke up with a lot of joy, and just a little sadness.

In Praise of Modesty

I have been intending for some time to put down a few words about modesty. It's a quality I greatly admire, even realizing that it is not much admired, indeed too easily dismissed or overlooked in a culture where self-esteem has become the accepted *sine qua non* of a strong, healthy personality, and where boastfulness and self-promotion abound. Still, in my view, modesty is by no means incompatible with self-esteem. It is rather, a quieter manifestation of the same strong sense of self. To be modest does not mean to be meek or submissive—qualities for which it is easily mistaken—but instead to have a balanced understanding of one's place in the world and among one's fellow human beings.

The word itself derives from the Latin *modestus*, meaning temperate. It is related, of course, to words like moderate and moderation. We enjoy living in a moderate climate. It is no accident that to *moderate* a possibly stormy discussion means to keep the process moving smoothly; nor that to say, for example, that to do everything *in moderation* is considered sage advice. To be modest, seen in this light, is to follow the wisdom of the Buddhist Middle Path, avoiding excess in either direction. It is not, as my friend the abbot of our nearby monastery nicely puts it, to be a doormat. It is not to be average, or even mediocre.

I like modest people—the kind of people who do not need to pretend to be anything other than they are, and who live comfortably within the bounds of their abilities and desires. They tend to be polite, considerate, and respectful—more qualities that are met with skepticism and sometimes even scorn in a world where ruthless competitiveness gets you ahead. They live within modest means, leaving less heavy a footprint on this long-suffering planet. Their needs, too, are modest. In their relationships with their fellow beings, they are generous, thoughtful, compassionate.

It's the same with works of art of all kinds. I love movies that strike me as modest; not the huge blockbusters, but the quieter kind—the kind that looks at human beings and indeed the natural environment with a lingering gaze and less noise-some drama. I love the work of artists who content themselves with modest, sparing, sometimes ephemeral means. Those who share my love of art will understand my admiration for an artist like Richard Tuttle, for example, whose artworks are mostly ultra-small in scale and constructed of unpretentious materials; or Andy Goldsworthy, who (even if sometimes in monumental scale) makes subtle interventions in the natural environment, works that can blend easily with nature, or melt, or be washed out by the tide, or simply blown away.

In our compulsion to feel important and powerful, we humans too often feel the need to impress our fellow beings and leave our mark on the world. Better, in my view, to follow the path of modesty, and to leave not a trace.

Gratitude, Always

I was meditating this morning on gratitude... with gratitude for the multitude of blessings in my life. For life itself; for a still healthy body, even with age; for the aches and pains that attest to the body's natural self-healing powers and remind me to take care of this vehicle that has served me so well for so many years; for the love of family and friends and the smiles of strangers; for a brain that has allowed me to write so much good sense—along with a great deal of nonsense—and continues to function, though perhaps not so efficaciously as before; for the material comforts and conveniences I am privileged to enjoy; for the infinite wonders of nature...

I found myself ending up with gratitude for the senses, still sharp enough to enjoy the aroma and taste of the food that I eat, the glass of wine that I drink in the evening; the sense of touch, the warmth of the blanket on my knees as I sit in meditation, the cushion that supports my rear end; the eyesight that allows me not only to marvel at the beauty of the garden outside our window but also to read—and write—the words I love. I ended up unable to resist a beatific smile as my ears began to tune in to the striking contrast between the deep, vibrating bass of Jake's snores as he slept on the bed close by and the high, piercing notes of the songbird in the pepper tree outside, the one resting peacefully in his dreams, the other already awake and celebrating the dawn.

So much to be grateful for. Much better this than to grouse about the effects of the advancing years on body and mind, let alone the dire state of the nation and the equally dire state of the world! I have discovered that gratitude is itself a kind of refuge—a refuge where I can always go to rest and heal from whatever trivial distraction besets me. Breathe in with awareness, breathe out with thanks...

Expanding Perception

Begin by bringing the attention to the breath, resting in attention on how it enters the body... how it fills and refreshes the body... how it leaves. Take as much time as you need to get comfortable with the breath.... Remind yourself of this: there's nothing to do, nowhere to go. Be fully present with the simple act of breathing...

Once you have made friends with the breath, bring your attention to the definition of the body, alert to the space that immediately surrounds and touches it... aware of the definition of each finger, of the hands... aware of the definition of the wrists and arms... the shoulders and the back of the neck... the head, concentrating on where its contour meets with the space that immediately surrounds it... the shape of the ears, the nose, the shape of the jaw, the cheeks... the eyelids... aware of the curve of the scalp at top of the head, the hair...

Bring the attention down to the back of the neck, the shoulders and the back, aware, again, of where the contours meet the air around you, the whole area of the back... breathing until you are comfortable in this awareness... and, taking your time, follow the same process with the front of the torso... the hips... the legs... the feet and toes... breathing quiet and steady as you hold your attention on the outer definition of the entire body, all at once...

When you're comfortable with the outer definition, exactly where each part of the body ends and the surrounding space begins, bring your attention to the space within, the mind now fully commensurate with the inner spaces of the body ... until you are comfortable in awareness of both the body within and the body without together, as one... the mind commensurate with the entire body, inside and out, breathing...

Breathing in this awareness, breathing it out, tell yourself: *may I be happy*, letting happiness permeate the entire body as you breathe... *may I be free from stress and pain*... releasing all tension in the body, breathing in, breathing out: *may I be free from trouble*... *may I be free from animosity*... releasing all hatred, all anger from the heart... *may I be free from oppression*... *may I look after myself with ease.*

The mind is commensurate with the entire body, commensurate with every nook and cranny, every fold and wrinkle... Breathing gently... breathing in restful attention...

Now expand the attention to include the space that immediately surrounds you, reaching out and breathing into the space just beyond the confines of the body... the mind no longer *me*, the mind greater than *self* as you breathe... And expanding ever outward to include those closest to you, those you love... including them with goodwill, with gratitude: *may they be happy*...

Now allow the mind to expand in ever-widening circles to include people you know less well, and people you like... and people you don't know very well at all... expanding the reach of the mind with goodwill to include even people you don't like: *may they, too, find happiness*... and now people you don't know at all, people everywhere, throughout the world... and still further to include all living beings, all in one single mind-space...

Breathing nothing but goodwill...

Imagine the mind reaching out to include not only all beings but the planet itself... breathing slowly to embrace the earth's atmosphere and further, as far as you can imagine in the universe beyond... all mind... all one... breathing quiet and steady in the vast expanse of mind... no borders, no horizons, pure space everywhere, in all directions... pure mind

Reaching all the way out to infinity...

Where you come to rest, embracing everything in rapt attention...

And slowly, gently, in your own comfortable time, reel the mind back in, in slowly diminishing circles, back to the earth's atmosphere... the planet... your own neighborhood... the confines of your body... back to the definition of the body in the space it occupies... back to the body within, the whole body as mind, breathing... and back to the core of the body, back to the heart...

Breathing in, breathing out...

And finally, imagine the sound of the gong as it begins to resonate... resonating three times... and as the last sound of the gong recedes, still resonating, open your eyes... and bring the body back to rest quietly in attention to the space around you.

Depression, Part II

This is a follow-up to an earlier discussion I had with my doctor a while ago regarding the low-grade depression I was experiencing. It is certainly age-related. Several friends of my age—and some of them younger—have told me of similar experiences. It's partly the frequency and ease with which fatigue can take over, partly a lack of motivation to do the things I normally do with pleasure, partly a fit of low spirits and general malaise. (My father, toward the end of his life, used to call it his "dumping syndrome"—as good a name for it as any).

My good doctor, a very lovely young woman who listens well and responds with measured good sense, asked back then if I'd care to consider a medication to help me out. My first instinct was to decline. I dislike medications of all kinds, even those I'm persuaded I need to take to regulate purely physical problems with thyroid and prostate—another manifestation of age. To resort to pharmacology to help me with emotional distress seemed unthinkable. What, me? Who has learned to take care of my inner life with thoughtful self-examination in the daily meditation practice I have pursued for more than twenty-five years? The very thought seemed shameful, offensive. I have never had a taste for even "natural" remedies like marijuana and its byproducts.

What I thought were good intentions, however, began to falter when the mood continued to manifest in my life. The next time I spoke to the doctor, a month or so ago, I decided to swallow my pride and follow her suggestion. At least I could give it a try. A blow to my ego, perhaps, but really, what harm could it do? She gave me a prescription for something called Wellbutrin. I started taking the pills with some anxiety about possible insomnia, weight loss, and other reported side effects but noticed nothing untoward. I learned, too, that a respected friend had recently started with the same medication and with the same sense of shame and offended pride. I know him as an experienced therapist possessed of a finely tuned understanding of human nature, a healer, a man as evolved in his consciousness as I flatter myself to be. Despite his reservations, he told me, the preliminary results seemed good. He was pleased to have started.

It is now a month since I began taking the pills I had a telephone appointment with my doctor yesterday to discuss the results and was able to tell her truthfully that I had indeed noticed an improvement in my mood, an increased lightness of being, a spring in my step that had too long been absent. Importantly, I had also experienced a return of the motivation to get on with what, aside from family, is the most important in my life: I am back to getting some writing every day and am close to finishing the revisions to these essays I have been thinking to publish as a book. Despite my reluctance to attribute all this to the little pill, I swallow every day with my breakfast—along with my pride!—they do seem to be working their pharmaceutical magic. I am grateful for the help and am happy to share my experience with others who might be as reluctant as myself. It may be that you, too, are among them…

The Dead

To give myself good cheer on this gloomy morning in Southern California, I meditated on the names of the dead.

The list includes every person who ever existed on this earth who is no longer alive. It includes Buddha and Jesus Christ and Mohammed, Confucius and Marcus Aurelius; it includes Cleopatra and Julius Caesar and Atilla the Hun and Alexander the Great; it includes St. Augustine and Edward the Confessor and Joan of Arc; it includes Michelangelo and Raphael and Botticelli and Dante; it includes Chaucer and Shakespeare and Henry VIII and all six of his six wives; it includes every one of the sixteen French Louis; it includes Queen Elizabeth I and, now, just recently, the long-reigning Queen Elizabeth II; it includes Milton and Wordsworth and Coleridge and Percy Bysshe Shelley, Lord Byron and Schiller and Goethe; it includes Bach and Beethoven and Brahms, along with Mozart and Tchaikovsky and Stravinsky; it includes Sojourner Truth and Harriet Tubman and Frederick Douglass; it includes Dostoyevsky and Tolstoy and Victor Hugo and Balzac and Flaubert, Charles Dickens and Emily Bronte and Jane Austen; Emily Dickinson and Melville, Edgar Allan Poe and Mark Twain; it includes Charles Baudelaire and Arthur Rimbaud and Stéphane Mallarmé; it includes Karl Marx and Sigmund Freud; it includes Marie Curie and Amelia Earnhardt; it includes Kaiser Wilhelm and the Tsar Nicholas II of Russia and all the Kings George and Edward of England; it includes Adolf Hitler and Goebbels and Goering and Himmler; it includes Churchill and Eisenhower and Stalin; it includes Mahatma Gandhi and Nelson Mandela; it includes Auden and Eliot and James Joyce and Andre Gide and Thomas Mann; it includes Picasso and Braque and Duchamp; it includes Willem de Kooning and Philip Guston and Helen Frankenthaler and Louise Bourgeois; it includes John Kennedy and Bobby Kennedy and Martin Luther King Jr.; it includes Jesse Owens and Muhammad Ali; it includes my mother and father and sister and my mother-in-law and my father-in-law and my stepmother-in-law.

It includes everyone who is no longer here with us on earth.

I ended my meditation taking note that I am here, still alive, and grateful for that. I am aware that my time will be coming soon enough.

D-Day

Today, June 6, 2024, marks the 80th anniversary of D-Day. As always on this day, I think with sadness of those thousands of lives lost on the beaches of Normandy; with honor and amazement at the courage of those young men who waded onshore, faced with the barrage of lethal Nazi gunfire; and with gratitude for the countless sacrifices that would lead to the rescue of the world from the menace of fascism—for a time, at least. At a time when the same menace is rife today in the form of actual and aspiring authoritarian leaders in all parts of the world, it is sad that we have learned so little from the past. Too many Americans—too many of us—have forgotten the meaning of that sacrifice by our compatriots, even now welcoming the prospect of authoritarian rule by a man no less deranged and intoxicated with power than the one who managed to inspire our enemies back then—a man comparably empowered by cowardly toadies and the belief in lies broadcast by propaganda. Today we are again confronted with the spectacle of a legal system buckling beneath the weight of shameless, outright, contemptuous violation.

There is another lesson still unlearned from that dark and all too recent past: the futility of war as a means to resolve differences between nations, whether territorial or ideological. In little more than a century, we have witnessed two great wars and countless smaller but no less deadly conflagrations. They have achieved nothing but widespread destruction, misery, death, and often a return to the *status quo ante*. But there are still men—yes, sadly, almost exclusively men—whose overweening ego drives whole nations into conflict.

I would have wished to mark this D-Day with a celebration of the peace and mutual understanding those men fought for. Instead, I read of universal discontent, intolerance, and abuse of power. Eight years old at the time of the Normandy invasion, protected from the ravages of war in the quiet country village where I lived—but no more than a hundred miles from the battleground—I grieve the failure of our collective memory and our essential humanity no less than the dreadful loss of human life that day. Our species seems bent on, first, the elimination of other members of our human tribe... and then on self-destruction. We are a very odd bunch of creatures indeed. Myself included.

Good news!

Laguna Beach, CA
Sunday, 28 July 2024

As I read through these pages for what I hope will be one last time, I have been noticing, with some sadness, how frequently I have been reflecting with bleak thoughts on the situation in America, on the mood of its people, and the politics of the moment. It has now been more than sixty years since I first crossed the Atlantic, fifty years since I became an American citizen. How everything has changed since the heady days of the 1960s and the struggle for personal freedom on so many fronts.

And then, in that light, what a difference a single week can make! A single week and a handful of minutes, to be precise. Last Sunday, at the start of the hour of meditation with my sitting group, we swore that we would avoid politics in our hour's discussion afterward. Inevitably, though, towards the end of our session, we fell into the trap. Something—I forget how it happened—led us into thoughts about the just-ended, loudly triumphant Republican convention that was buoyed by the recent assassination attempt on Trump (and the bandage on his ear!) and the dreadful feeling of approaching disaster that our little group shared as we contemplated the prospect of the country electing an aging, demented Trump, as boastful, cruel, and bullying as ever, along with a newly minted Vice President no less harsh than himself. With as vulnerable a target as a visibly aging

President Biden refusing to step aside, there was a growing sense of the inevitability of a Republican seizure of every branch of government.

I left our meeting with this doom hanging over me like the heaviest of clouds, even more pessimistic than I have been feeling in recent weeks. Got into the car to drive home, and the radio station I had been listening to before resumed as soon as the engine turned. Then, within moments, the news came through. President Biden had finally decided to step aside! Moments later came the follow-up news: he had endorsed Kamala Harris, his Vice President, as the best candidate to follow him in office!

Most of us, I think, had been expecting chaos. I had even been welcoming the prospect. Chaos, I thought, is sometimes what is needed before finding a good way forward. Chaos, though, is not what we got. Instead, within hours it seemed, Kamala Harris had stepped forward, glowing with optimistic confidence, taking charge of the situation with a big, joyful laugh and a few inspiring words. Later, in a nationally broadcast speech, she left no doubt about her intention to address the cancer of Trumpism, win the presidency, and usher the nation forward into a buoyant future.

I can hardly describe the elation and relief that I felt. Finally, the battle for the soul of this country was no longer between two old men, one of them angry, litigious, vengeful, with nothing to propose but further benefits for the rich at home and concession to tyrants abroad; the other a truly good-hearted man, politically skillful, successful beyond all expectations in his time in office, but now, sadly… old. Here, it seemed, all of a sudden, was a new, eloquent champion for human rights of all kinds, a truly Joyful Warrior, a Black and Asian American woman whose personal charisma shone forth at her every appearance.

I know—she knows, all of America knows—that this is not the end of the battle, but at least it is what Churchill called the end of the beginning.

She knows—and stresses constantly—that there is work to do if we are to avoid slipping back decades into a murky past and move forward instead into a promising future. But she is already inspiring thousands of others to help with that work, and others still to donate the money needed with unprecedented success. Better yet, with the courageous concession of Joe Biden, she was able to put a pin in that inflated balloon with which Trump and his Republicans left their convention and the whole party deflated, flat-footed, armed thus far with nothing but inane personal threats and insults to slow her progress. Policies? They have none that are not wildly unpopular with the majority of voters. Stuck with misogyny, not-so-covert racism and undisguised hostility, they look, as the Vice-Presidential candidate aptly put it, simply weird.

    I posted a picture on social media the day following the Biden announcement. It showed Kamala Harris letting loose with a great, genuine laugh, her eyes shining with both humor and defiance. Within hours of posting, 250 of my social media friends had responded to the image with unalloyed delight. For the first time in what seems like years, I am feeling unutterably relieved and hopeful for a more enlightened future. It is a good moment to be saying goodbye to this book and, myself, moving forward into… who knows what.

Envoi

There's a French literary term that has, to my knowledge, no exact equivalent in English: *Envoi*. It's a coda, a sending off, a conclusion, often the final stanza of a traditional ballad. A way of leaving it all behind.

It's only as I reach the final page of this collection that a title comes to mind. I thought of several along the way. For a while, there was *Essayettes*, describing its contents for what they were—not long or coherent enough to be called *Essays*, though I often had in mind and sometimes referred to a book I have long honored, the *Essais* of Michel de Montaigne. For a while, I entertained the notion of *Vignettes* or *Bagatelles*. It may seem odd that I kept returning to French models, but most of my literary studies from my earliest student days were in French literature, so that's not too surprising. I also considered the possibility of *Thoughts*, with another favorite French text in mind: Blaise Pascal's *Pensées*. Most of Pascal's writings are brief, like my own, and all of them are essays in the sense that they are *attempts* to get to the heart of things. I used "Getting to the heart of things" for many years as the epithet for my long-running blog, *The Buddha Diaries,* and the same phrase is also a key part of the mission statement I once wrote, in the attempt to encapsulate and define my greater purpose in life.

All of which was on my mind as I went through the many different versions of a possible title. I settled on the one I eventually chose, *A Piece of My Mind*, because it suggests something less pretentious than those other high-minded literary references. The rambling, not especially profound thoughts, memories, stories, dreams, and fragments of social or political commentary that populate these pages seem to me a good deal less serious than an essay but are rather more personal, conversational, and a little more intimate in tone and intention. I think of these pieces of writing as throwaways, a way of talking to a good friend about what happens to be on my mind at any given moment. I readily concede that they may be of no interest to no one other them myself—but hopefully also to that good friend.

When all's said and done, it's ridiculous to sit here trying to defend them. They are what they are; this, that and the other, just short pieces of writing, remnants salvaged from the wastebasket of a writer who is feeling his age and is vain enough to want to compile something of a record of his work, no more… and certainly no less.

www.ingramcontent.com/pod-product-compliance
Lightning Source LLC
LaVergne TN
LVHW061608070526
838199LV00078B/7210